The **ELECTRIC FOOTBALL™ WISHBOOK**
Sports Game Christmas Catalog Pages 1955 - 1988

Earl Shores   Roddy Garcia   Michael Kronenberg

Copyright © 2017 One Way Road Press
All rights reserved
ISBN: 978-0-9892363-3-1
onewayroadpress.com

This book is dedicated to all of us who had our Electric Football dreams inspired and furthered by a Christmas catalog page. Through these beautiful images we can still reach back and touch that wonderful time when the "Greatest Games" were played on our living room floors.

Acknowledgements

We are so grateful for the support we've received through these many years. Every type of interaction we've had – emails, Facebook comments, conversations at conventions, phone calls, even those long ago handwritten letters – has meant a lot to us. Your belief in our work has led us farther into the publishing world than we ever dreamed possible.

And without the generosity and belief of Norman Sas and Lee Payne, and continued support from the Sas, Payne, and Modica families, we would have hung up our Electric Football cleats a long time ago.

In the present, we are indebted to Doug Strohm and Tudor Games for keeping Electric Football alive and vibrant, and also for giving the game a promising future that includes the NFL. Having Tudor Games – the home of Electric Football – be a supporter and advocate of our work is an honor beyond words. Just in case that wasn't clear…yes, NFL Electric Football games and teams are available in 2017 from:

tudorgames.com

1969 Aldens

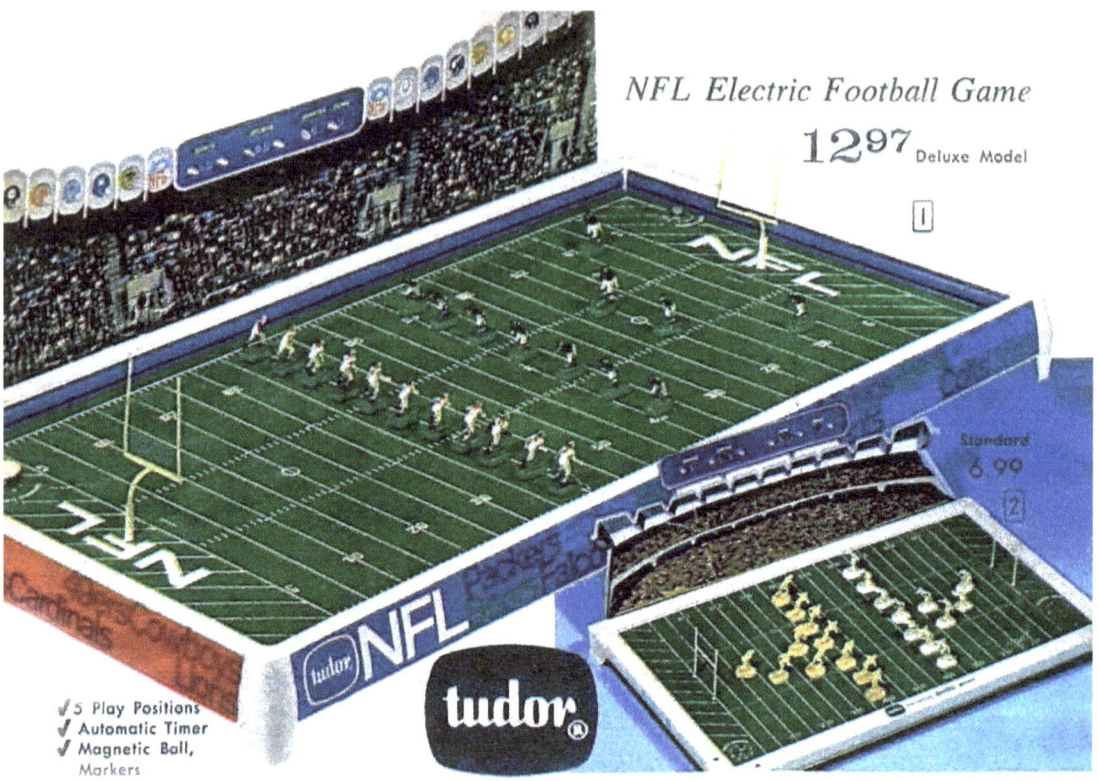

NFL Electric Football Game
12.97 Deluxe Model

Standard **6.99**

- 5 Play Positions
- Automatic Timer
- Magnetic Ball, Markers

tudor

Electric Football in Carrying Case **9.97**

1 DELUXE ELECTRIC NFL Game by Tudor. Numbered Cleveland Browns and N. Y. Giants recreate actual game. Automatic timer starts, stops with each play. Speed control, magnetic ball. Down and 10-yd. marker with chain. Scoreboard. Field: 37¾x20¼x3-in. 110-120V. UL Listed.
E85 Y 7417E—Mail./Exp. Shipping weight 10 lb.... **12.97**

2 TUDOR ELECTRIC FOOTBALL GAME—same as above but smaller field: 26½x15½x1¾-in. UL Listed. Mailable.
85 Y 7418E—Shipping weight 8 lb.................. **6.99**

3 NFL PRO-FOOTBALL by Ideal. Fans mastermind game! Offense makes runs, passes; defense tackles, intercepts. 22 movers, football, field, down markers, dice, rule book.
85 Y 7421—Mail. Shipping weight 3 lb............. **4.98**

4 NFL COMPUTER Quarterback Football by Transogram. Computer gives, play, ball position, score. 16 quarterbacks compete. Clocks for time, period, score. "D" Batt. below.
85 Y 7422—Plastic. Shipping weight 2 lb. 3 oz......... **9.97**
847 Y 6390—"D" Batteries for above. 1 lb. 11 oz, 6 for **99c**

5 NFLPA ELECTRIC FOOTBALL in decorated carrying case. Choose and change players with 48 red, white and blue name tabs. Molded styrene offensive players, molded magnetic football. Photo and autograph library of key NFL Players Association members included. Steel. 115V, AC.
E85 Y 7419E—Mail./Exp. Shipping weight 9 lb...... **9.97**

6 PRO-BOWL 3-D football game by Marx. Live action as simple or strategically complex as desired. Line-up offensive, specialist players on 4x8-ft. vinyl field. Mechanical runner. Quarterback-Passer-Kicker, Wheeled Line Backers.
85 Y 7420E—Real gridiron accessories. Mail. Wt. 7 lb. **8.97**

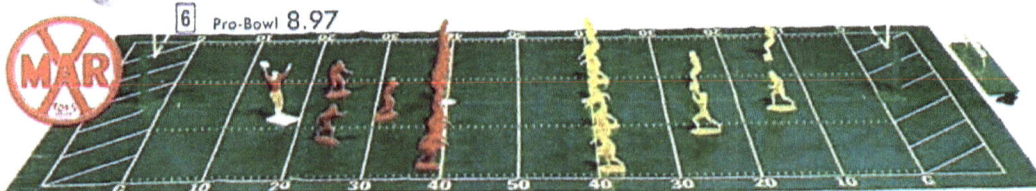

Pro-Bowl **8.97**

Introduction

Welcome to the first ever *Electric Football*™ *Wishbook*, a compilation of Electric Football Christmas catalog pages covering the years 1955-1988. The obvious stars of the *Wishbook* are the pages from Sears and Montgomery Ward, the retailers who ruled the U.S. mail order marketplace during this unique period. But Sears and Ward weren't the only retailers who understood Electric Football's appeal and popularity. J.C. Penney, Spiegel, and Aldens all produced fantastic looking catalog pages that make major contributions to the *Wishbook*.

The *Wishbook* is not a comprehensive collection of pages. In the early days of Electric Football most Christmas catalogs pictured the game in black and white. And it usually wasn't given any special presentation, being just another toy on a page with many other toys (see page 4). So we made a conscious decision not to tie up too much of our valuable *Wishbook* real estate with monochrome images. We felt it was important to tell the Christmas catalog story in the most colorful way possible.

Electric Football first appeared in the Sears, Montgomery Ward, and Spiegel Christmas catalogs in 1955. Sears and Ward sold Gotham Pressed Steel models, while Spiegel sold the Tudor Tru-Action No. 500. Gotham maintained its Christmas catalog dominance throughout the 1950's, with both Sears and Ward remaining loyal to the Bronx-based toy maker.

But the 1960's would usher in significant change for Electric Football, driven by the rising stature of the NFL and the NFL Electric Football license that Gotham acquired after Tudor turned it down in early 1960. From here on Tudor and Gotham engaged in an intense competition for Christmas catalog visibility, one that spurred both companies to innovate and create new Electric Football features on a yearly basis. This produced a Golden Age for Electric Football, a time when the evolution of the game was documented annually by the Christmas catalogs that arrived in our mailboxes. For those of us who grew up during this era few things have matched the wonder of turning a catalog page and seeing the Gotham Big Bowl (page 16) or the first Sears Super Bowl model (page 26).

By the late 1960's Electric Football was a "Featured Toy," not only in Christmas catalogs but also on store shelves. Tudor's early line of NFL games sold out completely, with retailers clamoring for more games than the company could make. This unmet demand caught the eye of other toy makers, and by the early 1970's there were four different companies selling Electric Football. Out of this four-way competition came some of the most dream-inducing Christmas catalog pages ever produced, with retailers even devoting multiple pages to the game.

Unfortunately the early 1970's brought an energy crisis, a recession, air hockey games, and worst of all for Electric Football, electronic gaming systems. Electric Football's struggles began mid-decade, with the declining influence of the game on full display throughout the Christmas catalog pages of the late 1970's. Not only were fewer models being sold, they were given less and less catalog space. This space squeeze continued throughout the 1980's as Electric Football reverted – at least in the Ward and J.C. Penney catalogs – to its 1950's status of being just another toy on the page. The 1988 Sears page is significant because it marked the last appearance of a Brooklyn-made Tudor Electric Football game in a Christmas catalog. (Superior Toy of Chicago took over the company and the Electric Football line in 1989.)

There is no Table of Contents in the *Wishbook*, only a comprehensive Game Index on page 75. That's because we discovered in our earliest drafts that the catalog page concept worked best as an old-fashioned slide show. Being able to wander from image to image and page to page without processing gobs of text seemed a more pure, and dare we say, childlike way of taking things in. And we think it makes a resounding case for finally getting Electric Football into the Toy Hall Of Fame. The sooner the better.

We hope the *Wishbook* brings back all of your wondrous Christmas morning dreams and memories.

Earl, Roddy, & Michael

1955 Montgomery Ward

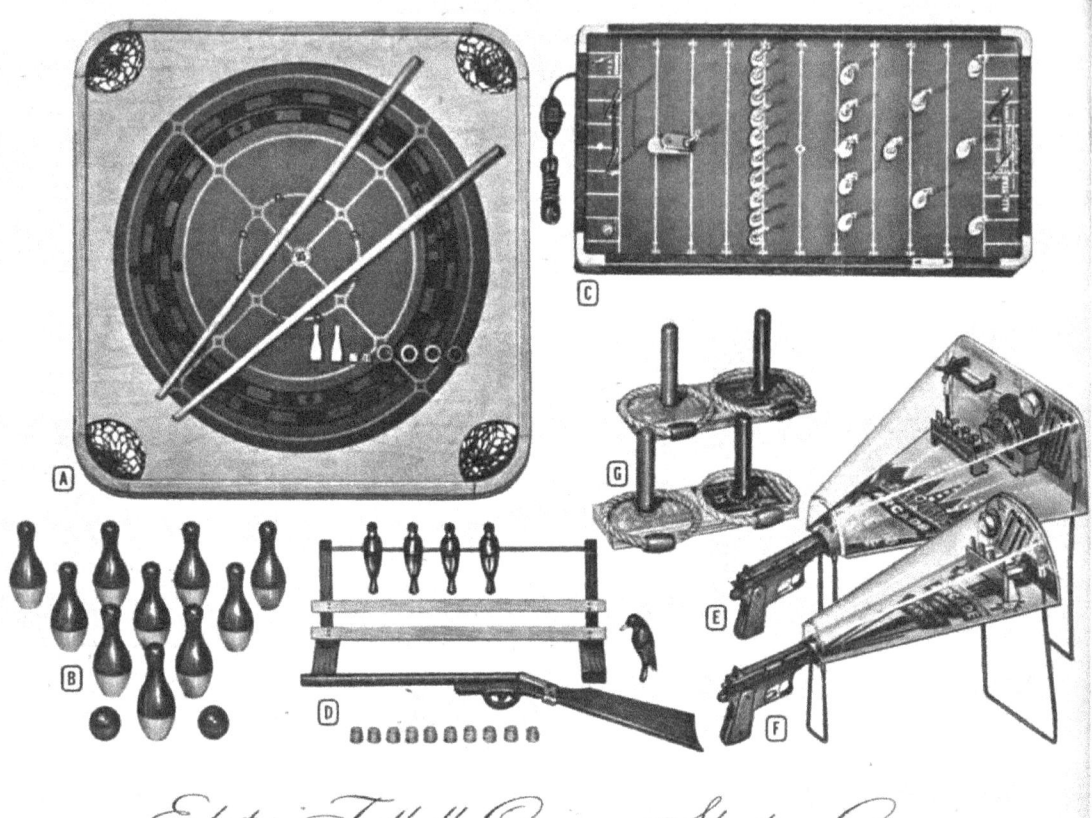

Electric Football, Carrom, Shooting Games

[A] 95-GAME DE LUXE CARROM BOARD. Everything you need for 95 different games—Crokinole, Carroms, Ten Pins and many others. Smooth 3-ply wood surface in hardwood frame. 28½ in. sq., nicely finished and lacquered. Printed in attractive colors. Crokinole panel on one side, Backgammon and Checker Boards on other. Reversible net pockets, rounded corners. Green felt cushion on Carrom side. 2 felt-tipped cues, 29 hardwood rings, playing pieces. *Mail.*
48 T 715 MO—Instructions. Ship. wt. 10 lbs... **8.98**

48 T 714 MO—85-GAME CARROM BOARD. Similar to (A) above but has equipment for 85 games. Nicely finished wood, 28½ in. sq. 3-ply playing panel with printed diagram in hardwood frame. Instr. 2 cues. *Mailable.* Ship. wt. 9 lbs. **7.89**

EXTRA HARDWOOD CARROM RINGS for boards.
48 T 747—29 Carrom rings. Ship. wt. 6 oz... **50c**

[B] COLORFUL PLASTIC DUCK PINS. Set 'em up —knock 'em down. Use indoors or outdoors, alone or with an opponent. Can be played like real bowling. 10 plastic red and yellow pins, 5 in. high. 2 colored hardwood balls. Boxed.
48 T 865—Ship. wt. 1 lb. 3 oz............ **1.25**

[C] ELECTRIC FOOTBALL GAME. True-to-life football. Players race down 28½x15⅛-in. gridiron activated by hidden electric motor. Plays run from any formation, ball is kicked, passed. Masonite Presdwood surface, steel frame. Vibrating motor, cord. On-Off switch, 110-120V, AC, UL Appr'd. 22 players, kicker-passer, goal posts, markers, numbers for players, magnetic footballs. Usually retails for about $7.
48 T 820 M—Instr. *Mail.* Wt. 3 lbs. 12 oz... **5.69**

[D] CROW SHOOT. Shoot crows off steel wire perched on wood fence 15⅝x7½ in. 5 plastic crows. 14½-in. steel barrel "pop" gun. Corks.
48 T 844—Instr. Ship. wt. 1 lb. 2 oz........ **1.69**

[E] [F] ARCADE AUTOMATIC PISTOL SHOOTING RANGES. Test your aim. Each has self-feeding, automatic pistol, permanently attached, fires steel balls. Steel base for each range enclosed in transparent molded plastic. 20 in. long.
(E) MOTOR DRIVEN GALLERY. Wind it up. Hit spinning ducks, ring bell, turn propeller.
48 T 902—12½ in. wide. Ship. wt. 4 lbs. 12 oz. **4.79**
(F) GALLERY WITHOUT MOTOR. No spinning targets ... otherwise same as above.
48 T 901—7½ in. wide. Ship. wt. 2 lbs. 10 oz. **2.75**

[G] RING TOSS. Takes skill to toss rings over 4 wood posts. 2 teams may compete. 2 wood bases, 3⅝x10 in. long; 4 rope rings, wood grips.
48 T 833—Instructions. Wt. 1 lb. 11 oz....... **85c**

[H] DENNIS THE MENACE MISCHIEF KIT. Give child harmless outlet for his energy. Here is a box loaded with mischief-mad tricks. Rubber "razzer," trick tie, imitation ink blot, many more.
48 T 917—Instr. incl. Ship. wt. 1 lb. 5 oz..... **1.75**

[J] MAGNETIC GLOBAL AIR RACE with authentic 8-in. world globe. Exciting to the finish. Winner must circle globe. 4 magnetized airplanes in different colors. 4-bladed propeller on spinner at base of globe indicates hours of flight, fuel needed, chances. Money, fuel drums, chance cards.
48 T 702L—2-4 players. Instr. Wt. 3 lbs. .. **4.45**

[K] PITCH 'EM HORSESHOE GAME. 2 solid metal bases 11¾ in. square, sturdy steel posts. 4 wire reinforced rubber horseshoes 5¾ in. long.
48 T 737—Instr. Ship. wt. 2 lbs. 8 oz........ **1.10**

GAMES ON THESE PGS. AVAILABLE
UNTIL OCT. 1, 1956.

234 WARDS BA2

1955 Spiegel

1956 Sears

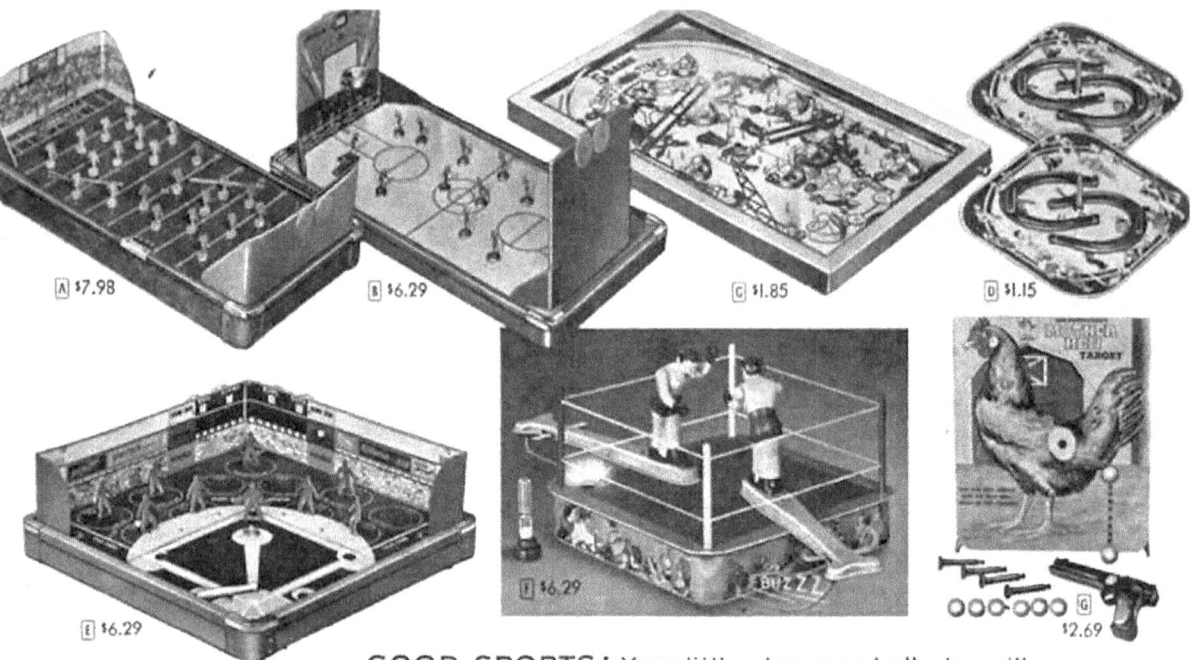

GOOD SPORTS! Your little playground all-star will welcome these action-packed games that test his scoring skills

[A] **Electro-Magnetic Football Game.** Masonite Presdwood playing surface. Plastic players, kickers and passers. 2 magnetic balls, goal posts. For 110-120-volt, 60-cycle AC. UL approved. 28½x15⅛x8 in. high. Rules included.
79 N 0236—Shpg. wt. 7 lbs. **$7.98**

[B] **Electric Basketball.** All the thrills of real basketball. Masonite Presdwood surface, steel frame. 2 backboards 110-120-volt, 60-cycle AC UL listed. 5 red, 5 blue plastic players. 1 magnetic ball 1 shooter. 15½x28⅜x2⅜-in.
79 N 0309—Shpg. wt. 7 lbs. **$6.29**

[C] **Happi-Time Game Board** 5 games in 1. Bagatelle, Pennants, 21, Put 'n' Take, Baseball. Automatic feed, reload. Steel spring shooter, traps, 10 balls. Composition board, wood frame, glass cover 18x21x1 in.
49 N 144—Wt. 3 lbs 8 oz. **$1.85**

[D] **Original Pitch-em-Horseshoes.** Two pairs of molded, steel-reinforced 5¾-in. rubber horseshoes. Two lithographed steel plates, 11⅝ inches square with removable pegs. Designed for use almost anywhere; indoors or out. Add a set to your list.
49 N 174—Wt. 2 lbs 10 oz. **$1.15**

[E] **New! Push Button Magnetic Baseball.** Push button, pitcher throws curves, fast balls—gives you big league thrills. Masonite Presdwood and steel playing surface. 9 sturdy metal players, 3 magnetic balls. Score sheet, rules. 18⅞x18x6½ inches.
79 N 0215—Shpg. wt. 6 lbs. **$6.29**

[F] **New! Knockout.** Hold your own title bouts. Sturdy boxers move in every direction; lefts, rights controlled by players. One on the button, you're down for the count, buzzer sounds, light glows. Real bell, timer. Metal base with rubber feet. Operates on flashlight battery incl. 12x12x6½ in. high.
49 N 284—Shpg wt 3 lbs. 8 oz. **$6.29**

[G] **New! Mother Hen Target Game.** Sharpens up the shootin' eye of even the youngest sharpshooter. Target lithographed in full color. 8 plastic eggs go into funnel inside the target, every time the aim is true an egg drops in the basket. 17x14x2-in. metal target, 4 darts, black plastic gun.
49 N 198—Wt. 2 lbs. 12 oz. **$2.69**

New! Burrowes Pool Tables In 6 Sizes .. Lively Action For Son, Dad

Packed with professional features. Four largest sizes have bed and leg leveling devices, cloth-covered cushions and select maple corners and legs. Bed and leg leveling devices adjust to give you a level playing surface. Special bed-leveling device lets you accurately adjust the *entire* playing surface. All sizes have "Roll-A-Way" rails that return balls to end tray. Handy rod marker. Warp-resistant Masonite Presdwood top has heavy green cloth covering. Resilient cushions. Rounded corners. Double-braced legs fold easily for storage. Husky hardwood frame. 16 numbered, colored balls, 2 hardwood cues, racking triangle, instruction booklet. 5 largest sizes have counters. Shipped freight, express or truck, except 40-inch size, which is mailable.

Length	Width	Height	Diameter of Balls	Cue Lengths	Catalog No.	Shpg. wt.	Price
72 inches	40 in.	31 in.	1⅞ inches	48 inches	79 N M428	162 lbs.	$159.95
66 inches	33 in.	30 in.	1⅞ inches	44 inches	79 N M427	75 lbs.	98.95
54 inches	30 in.	30 in.	1½ inches	42 inches	79 N M426		59.95
50½ inches	28 in.	29 in.	1⅜ inches	36 inches	79 N M425	42 lbs.	39.95
44½ inches	25 in.	28 in.	1⅛ inches	36 inches	79 N M423	29 lbs.	21.95
40 inches	22½ in.	26 in.	1⅛ inch	32 inches	79 N 0422L	19 lbs.	12.95

Table Model Miniature Pool Table .. Fine Quality

Set up on a card or game table . . . you're ready to play! Return alley delivers balls conveniently to rack at end from pockets . . . no groping for "sunk" balls. Masonite Presdwood top covered with smooth, soft cotton flocking. Sturdy steel frame and legs . . . metal pockets and corner. Rubber cushions. Two rubber-tipped wood cue sticks; 15 numbered composition balls, 1⅜-inch diameter; one cue ball. Metal triangle rack. Over-all size: 30x17½x6½ inches high. Add it to your Easy Terms order, pay only 10% down. It's a gift your family will enjoy for many years.
79 N 0402L—Shipping weight 11 pounds........ **$8.79**

1958 Montgomery Ward

1962 General Merchandise

1962 Spiegel

New this Christmas

GOLFERINO
12.88

Play miniature golf on your table—9 holes with hazards!

Great new fun game for all the family! Full 9-hole miniature golf course you can play on table, floor—indoors, outdoors! Realistically molded, sturdy plastic layout ... complete with bridges, tunnels and exciting hazards. Players take turns pressing control button to make golfer swing club and hit ball. When ball goes in last hole, No. 9, bell rings and gold-colored loving cup pops up from ground! Includes rules, score cards. 22x23½ in.
R36 J 3349. Mailable. Shipping weight 6 lbs. 12.88

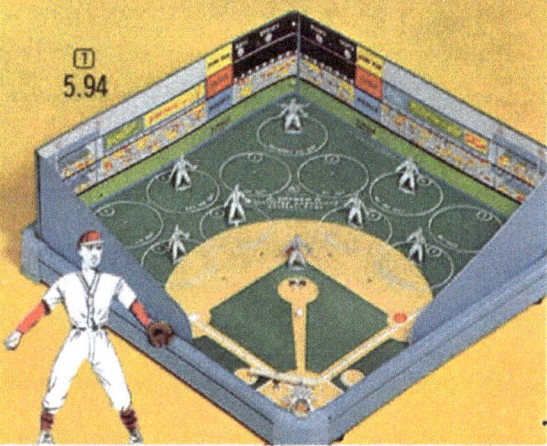
[1] 5.94

[2] 9.94

[3] 5.33

[1] **PUSHBUTTON BASEBALL.** Batter up ... play ball! Push button for pitch—fast, slow, inside or outside! Opponent releases spring-operated bat—gets walk, strike-out or hit. Scoreboard keeps count of balls, strikes, runs and outs. Sturdily made; steel fence, hardboard field. 3 magnetic balls, score sheet, baseball rules. Mailable.
R36 J 3318. Pushbutton, 19x19x6 in. high. Sh. wt. 8 lbs. .. 5.94
R36 J 3361. Electro-magnetic; 110-120V. AC. 22x22x7 in. (9 lbs.) 6.77

[2] **ELECTRIC HOCKEY GAME.** Fast action—just like the real game! You and your opponent guide forward, back and turn movements of 6 metal players of each team. Light flashes when score is made! Board keeps score and time. Three pucks included—1 magnetic, 1 regular, 1 marble—to vary action. Mechanical puck ejector. Plastic net; safety shield. Requires 2 "D" cell batteries, sold on page 324.
W36 J 3355. 20x35½ in. long. Mailable. Sh. wt. 14 lbs. 9.94

[3] **ELECTRIC ACTION FOOTBALL** ... more real than ever! Each team has kicker-passer who actually boots or passes ball. Match offensive and defensive strategy—run, block, tackle—even fumble! Electric vibration action moves players through lines. Molded 3-dimensional, 1½-in. tall players—24 in all. Metal frame and field. Down-marker and goal posts. On-off switch. About 27x16x2 inches high.
R36 J 3312. 110-120V. AC only. Mailable. Sh. wt. 6 lbs. .. 5.33

[4] **PUNCHY PALS** ... kiddies just love their playful antics! Poke 'em in the nose—push 'em, knock 'em down—they pop upright again for more! Inflatable heavy gauge plastic. Weighted bottoms.
35 J 3483. Dishonest John. 50 in. high. (3 lbs. 8 oz.) 3.44
35 J 3482. Captain Huffenpuff. 39 in. high. (3 lbs. 7 oz.) .. 2.66
35 J 3481. Beany Punchy. 27 in. high. (2 lbs. 10 oz.) 1.66

[4] 3.44

1.66

2.66

Lowest Budget Power Terms in history give you more buying power

1962 Sears

It's just like real football with plenty of body contact and broken field running. When the big 36x21-inch electrically-controlled field starts to vibrate, all of the 22 men are set in motion.

$12.44
National League Electric Football

Just like playing a real football game. Backfield men, carrying magnet-tipped football, try for first downs and TD's. Linemen can block and tackle. A spring catapult, used for kick-offs and passing, adds more realism... opposing team can intercept passes and take over. Offense controls the push button vibrator. The hardboard field is set in steel frame. Includes emblems, pennants, stick-on uniforms, goal posts, markers, metal scoreboard and rules. Operates on 110-120 volt, 60-cycle AC. UL listed.
79 N 404L—Shipping weight 13 lbs...$12.44

Electric Football on a 28x15-in. vibrating board — $7.66

Put all your football strategy into action with a team of miniature players that leap into motion when the switch is flipped on your electric vibrating field. Kicker passer sets up authentic plays. Ball can be kicked, passed and run. All 22 players block and tackle. Operates on 110-120 volt, 60 cycle AC. UL listed motor. Game also includes 2 magnetic balls. Hardboard field in steel frame, goals, markers.
79 N 236C — Shipping weight 7 pounds...$7.66

Foto-Electric Football on lighted gridiron — $5.44

Quarterback your own team! Viewer shows every play in motion... duplicates results, hard-hitting action and suspense of real football. Field with illuminated Play-viewer; offense and defense plays, scoreboard; dials for kicks, runbacks... all in box 18x13½x5 inches. Includes 11 plastic players. Play-viewer is UL listed, operates on 110-120 volt, 60 cycle AC-DC.
49 N 216 – Shipping weight 4 lbs. 2 oz...$5.44

Battery-operated Spinner Football — $2.66

The quarterback in this game is a battery-controlled spinner. Signal code numbers decide the plays. Wooden pegs keep score as the plastic football is moved up and down the 16x6-inch fiberboard field. Uses 1 "D" battery; order below.
79 N 367C — Shipping weight 2 lbs. $2.66
"D" Battery. Shipping weight each 4 oz.
79 N 4860... Each 16¢, 4 for 60¢

Electric Track Meet with moving men — $5.44

A switch at the starting gun for real-action. It starts mile, quarter mile or low hurdle races, setting 4 plastic trackmen moving around vibrating 15x26 in. board. Plastic over metal. 110-120v., 60 cy. AC. UL listed.
79 N 348C — Shipping weight 4 pounds...$5.44

Electric Cars race on 28x15-in. track — $6.88

Speedway auto racing in miniature. Four plastic cars whiz over the tricky four lane track... corner, pull away on the straights and speed over the finish line on the vibrating board. Hardboard in durable steel frame. Plug into any 110-120 volt, 60 cycle AC outlet. UL listed.
79 N 357C — Shipping weight 6 pounds...$6.88

Skill Drive magnetic Raceway Game — $1.66

Racing car fancier can take the wheel himself and maneuver sports car over a twisty course right on 10½x14 in. cardboard raceway. Two miniature plastic cars negotiate curves, bridges, run into road blocks. Player controls magnet underneath raceway.
49 N 383 — Shipping weight 1 lb. 8 oz...$1.66

1962 Montgomery Ward

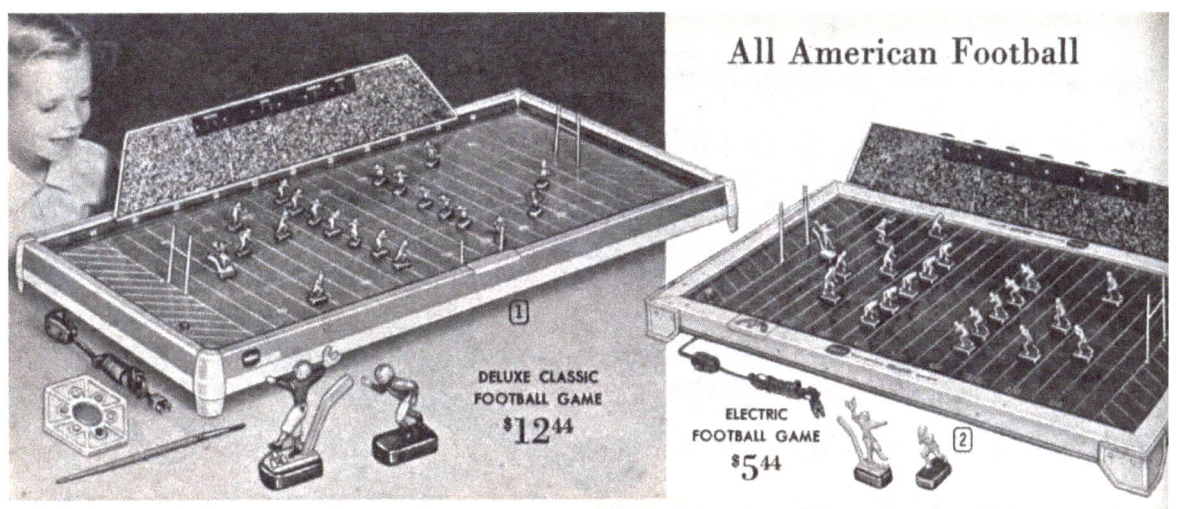

All American Football

① DELUXE CLASSIC FOOTBALL GAME $12.44

② ELECTRIC FOOTBALL GAME $5.44

Classic Action Games

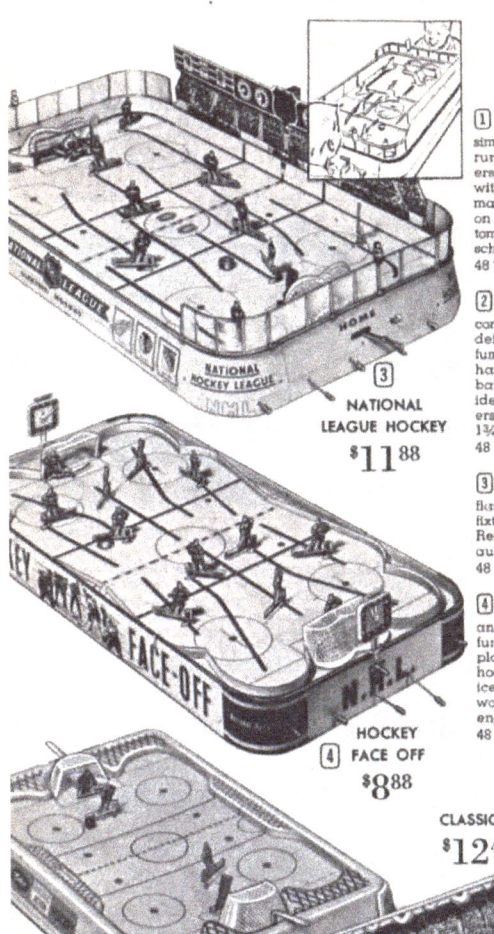

③ NATIONAL LEAGUE HOCKEY $11.88

④ HOCKEY FACE OFF $8.88

⑤ REMOTE CONTROL HOCKEY $5.88

⑥ CLASSIC ELECTRIC BASEBALL $12.44

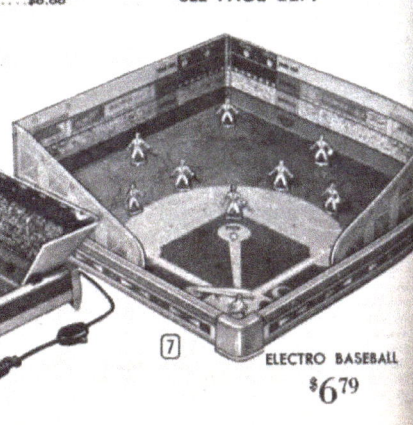

⑦ ELECTRO BASEBALL $6.79

① **Classic Electric Football Game.** Offensive and defensive 3-dimensional players, 34 of them, simulate the action of a real football game. They run, block, tackle, pass and kick like real players. Kicker-Passer for each team actually kicks with his foot, passes with his arm. Yardage, ball marker and even a 10 yard marker. Players run on new Vibra-action legs. Includes special "customizing" paint set to make-up teams in your school colors. 37¾x20¾x3 in.
48 T 1066 MO—Mail. Wt. 9 lbs. 8 oz......$12.44

② **Electric Football Game.** Five different 3-dimensional action posed players; make 2 complete teams. Linemen, ends, offensive and defensive backs run, block, tackle, pass and fumble ... make the game realistic. Each team has a Kicker-Passer that actually handles the ball like a real player. Press-on numbers to identify players. Yardage, ball and down markers help simulate actual game. About 26¼x15¼x 1¾ in. overall. Fun for ages 6-up.
48 T 741 M—Mailable. Ship. wt. 4 lbs.......$5.44

③ **All The Thrills Of Real Hockey.** New wide open play pattern—even behind nets. Red light flashes when goal is scored. Extra forward (and fixture) for last minute of play. Puck dropper. Realistic rink with rounded corners has bleacher audience. Abt. 36x21x9½ in. overall.
48 T 799 MO—Mailable. Ship. wt. 13 lbs...$11.88

④ **Fast Action Hockey Face Off.** An exciting game sure to delight any youngster on Christmas and every day of the year. A realistic action, fun filled game the whole family will enjoy playing. All players move along the ice as in real hockey. Defensemen can advance to center of ice. Plastic scoreboards at each end. Play the world's fastest sport with Dad or Mom for added enjoyment. About 36x18x4 in. overall. Mailable.
48 T 800 MO—Ship. wt. 9 lbs. 8 oz..........$8.88

⑤ **Electric Action Hockey Game.** Now the youngster in the family can enjoy the thrills of Hockey. Remote controlled electric action (battery operated) players make this game easy to operate. Requires 4 "D"-cell batteries (not included—see Page 345). Abt. 30x19½x3 in. overall. For ages 5-10.
48 T 801 MO—Mailable. Ship. wt. 5 lbs... $5.88

⑥ **Classic Electric Baseball Game.** Exclusive pistol-grip "Pitcher-Fielder" throws curves, fast balls, slow balls, fields grounders, makes put-out-throws. Players bat magnetic ball right or left handed, then true-to-life figures run or steal bases. Fielders catch flies, make double plays. Game can duplicate every baseball play. Follow regular baseball rules. World Series crowd in background. Abt. 23¾x23¾x3 in. high. For ages 9-up.
48 T 1065 M—Mailable. Ship. wt. 9 lbs. ..$12.44

⑦ **Electro-Magnetic Baseball** is the Big League of fun. It's "Batter-up" when players take positions. Push a button ... the mechanical pitcher hurls the ball ... batter hits ... magnetic ball adheres to field, players or fence to show whether it's a hit, strike-out or walk. Masonite field, metal frame, fences. Capacity Bleacher crowd. Electric motor is UL Approved. 9 players, balls, scoreboard, instructions, abt. 21x21x6 in. overall. Ages 5-up.
48 T 903 M—Mailable. Ship. wt. 7 lbs. 4 oz. $6.79

JUST SAY "Charge It"
SEE PAGE 227.

1963 Sears

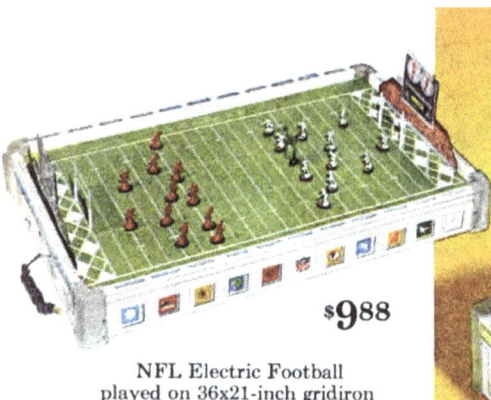

$9.88

NFL Electric Football
played on 36x21-inch gridiron

Running, blocking, passing, kicking .. you'll find all the fast action of real football right here on this big vibrating field. Set includes: 2 teams of 3-dimensional figures in color .. plus a separate kicker-passer. Workable scoreboards mounted at each end; goal posts, 3-man yardage marker, NFL plays and instruction sheet. The hardboard field is set in steel frame. Operates on 110-120-volt, 60-cycle AC only. UL approved.
79 N 401L—Shipping weight 12 pounds. $9.88

Watch these 3-dimensional football players go into action .. and run off exciting plays on a big de luxe gridiron

National League Electric Football $11.88

Two full teams in realistic on-the-move positions .. ready for you to paint with special paints and brush included

A vibrating coil in the field puts "a-c-t-i-o-n" in this game. All team players block, tackle, run for yardage and TD's .. even receive passes from the spectacular kicker-passer, using a magnetic-tipped football. Set up your offensive and defensive formations .. sit back and watch. Hardboard playing field, 36x21 in., set in steel frame.

Big grandstand section in center with workable scoreboards at each end. Includes pennants, goal posts, 3-man yardage marker, instructions and NFL plays. Coil and cord attached underneath board. Operates on 110-120-volt, 60-cycle AC only. UL approved.
79 N 105L—Shipping weight 13 pounds .. $11.88

$5.32

NFL Electric Football
played on 28x15-inch gridiron

Put all your football know how into action with these teams of 3-dimensional players. Flip the switch and they're in motion .. passing, kicking, blocking. Paint them in your favorite team colors with the paint and brush set included. Metal scoreboards, goal posts, kicker-passer, magnetic ball, yardage marker and instruction sheet with NFL plays. Hardboard field is set in steel frame. UL approved for 110-120-volt, 60 cycle AC.
79 N 141C—Shipping weight 6 pounds. $5.32

$4.99

Foto-Electric Football on lighted gridiron

Quarterback your own team. This viewer shows every play in motion .. duplicates all the hard hitting action and excitement of regular football games.
Includes: field with illuminated Play Viewer; offensive and defensive play cards; dials for kicks and runs in box measuring 18x13¾x5 inches. Play Viewer operates on 110-120-volt, 60-cycle AC-DC. UL approved.
49 N 216—Shipping weight 6 lbs. 8 oz. .. $4.99

$2.97 without batteries **$4.99** without batteries **$5.97**

Play New Vibro-Power Football on this 20x13-inch field

Here's a football game packed with fast moving excitement at a low cost. Plastic gridiron vibrates on battery power, sending players into plays and positions. Order 2 "D" batteries at right. 22 players are 3-dimensional plastic. Includes: kicker-passer, goal posts, instructions.
79 N 243C—Shpg. wt. 3 lbs. $2.97

Play all positions in Electro Magnetic Action Baseball

An electronic coil propels the pitching arm. At touch of a button you can pitch curves, slow and fast balls. Slam magnetic baseball into play with lever action bat. Hardboard base 19x19 in.; steel frame. 9 metal players. UL listed, 110-120-volt, 60-cycle AC.
79 N 418C—Shipping weight 6 lbs .. $5.97

Tap button to play Remote-control Battery-powered Baseball Game

Play ball! Control pitching and batting action with remote controls (order 4 "D" batteries below). Bat can be moved to right or left for switch hitting. Plastic field measures 30x20 inches. Includes: ball, metal pitcher, instructions. For 2 players.
79 N 350L—Shipping weight 5 pounds .. $4.99
79 N 4660—"D" Batteries. Wt. 4 oz. Ea. 16c; 4 for 60c

1963 Montgomery Ward

Deluxe Electric FOOTBALL GAME — $12.95

- Playing Board over 3 feet long
- 3-dimensional "sculpt-action" players simulate real-game action
- Offensive and defensive players run, block, and tackle
- Kicker-Passer for each team kicks with foot, passes with arm
- Paints and Press-on Numerals

[2] Electric Football $5.99

[3] Hockey Face-Off $9.47

[4] National League Hockey $12.99

[5] Bas-Ket $3.79

[6] Golferino $12.99

[7] Electric Baseball $12.95

[8] Electro-Magnetic Baseball $6.17

1964 Sears

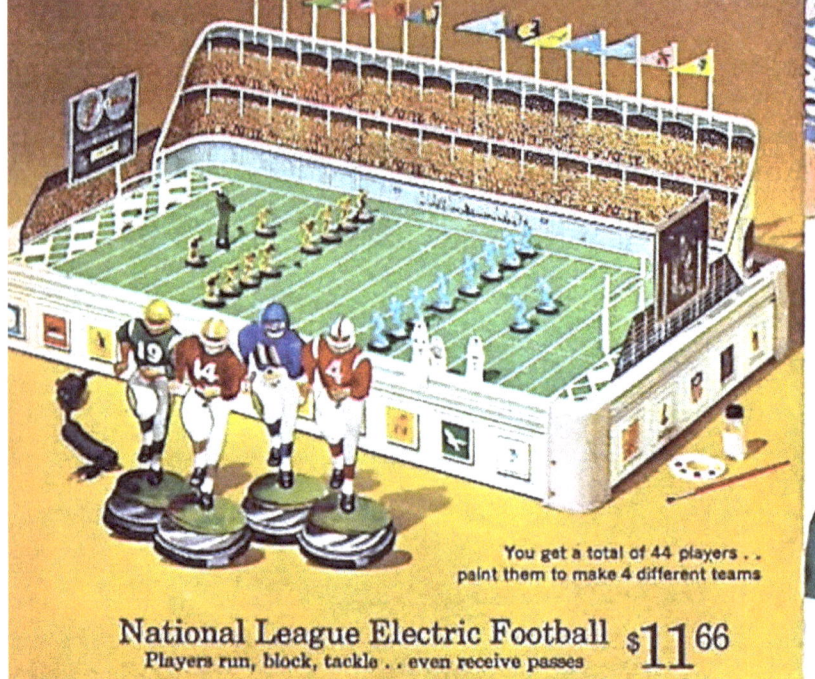

You get a total of 44 players.. paint them to make 4 different teams

National League Electric Football $11.66
Players run, block, tackle.. even receive passes

Set up your formations.. then watch these 3-dimensional players run off exciting plays on big 36x21-in. field. Vibrating coil in field keeps men in action. Spectacular kicker-passer actually throws and boots magnetic football.
Big center grandstand with workable scoreboards at each end. Set includes pennants, goal posts, 3 magnetic footballs, 3-man yardage marker, instructions and NFL plays. Paints and brush so you can paint players to make 4 different teams or offensive and defensive platoons. Hardboard field, steel frame. Cord, coil operate on 110-120-volt, 60-cy. AC. UL listed.
79 N 322L—Shipping weight 13 lbs. . $11.66

Call the plays.. end-run, off-tackle, forward pass or a "trick play." Your opponent tries to stop your advance

Pro Football by EMENEE
$9.33 without batteries

Exciting battery-powered game lets you call your own plays.. opponent tries to select right defense. Your "quarterbacking" makes football move along playing field.. and score.
Set includes flashing automatic penalty indicator, first down marker, scoreboard and down indicator. Plastic frame 26x10-in. Order 2 "D" batteries, above right on opposite page.
79 N 116C—Shipping weight 5 lbs. . . $9.33

NFL Electric Football Games

Big 36x21-inch gridiron

Here's all the rugged action of real football. Watch your 2 teams of 3-dimensional players fight it out.. 6 substitutes, the rest are "first-string." Magnetic ball. Separate kicker-passer.
Grandstand with 2 workable scoreboards, 4 pennants. Goal posts, 3-man yardage marker, NFL plays, instruction sheet. Steel-framed hardboard. 110-120-volt, 60-cycle AC. UL listed.
$9.88
79 N 328L—Shpg. wt. 11 lbs. .$9.88

29x15-inch NFL gridiron

Put your football know-how into action with these 2 teams of 3-dimensional players. Separate kicker-passer. Each team also has 2 substitutes.
Grandstand with scoreboard, 2 pennants. Goal posts, magnetic ball, yardage marker, NFL plays, instructions. Hardboard field, steel frame. 110-120-volt, 60-cy. AC. UL listed.
$5.44
79 N 331C—Shpg. wt. 6 lbs. .$5.44

Foto-Electric Football $5.88

Quarterback your own team. Lighted gridiron shows every play in motion.. all the action, suspense of top pro games.
"Hall of Fame" set includes offensive and defensive play cards, dials for kicks and runs, scoreboard. 19x14x5-in. box. Laminated cardboard. Play-Viewer operates on 110-120-v., 60-cy. AC. UL listed.
49 N 114C—Shipping wt. 4 lbs. .$5.88

$2.99

Jr. League Magnetic Baseball

True-to-life game situations spelled out on playing field. Plays determined by where magnetic ball stops. Remote pitching, batting plus unique "put-out" feature let little ball players improve their skills. 1 to 2 players. 19x19-in. Steel-framed hardboard.
79 N 321C—Shipping weight 4 lbs. .$2.99

1964 Montgomery Ward

1964 Aldens

1965 Sears

NFL Electric Football with 36x21-inch gridiron

All the exciting action of real football on this vibrating gridiron. Cross-buck, screen pass, end around and more. 2 teams of life-like 3-dimensional players clash while 6 substitutes wait to be called in. Separate kicker-passer, magnetic football, 3-man yardage marker, goal posts. Metal grandstand with 2 workable scoreboards, flying pennants. Steel-framed hardboard. Plays and instruction sheet. UL listed, 110-120-v., 60-c. AC. Shpg. wt. 12 lbs.
79 N 301L............$9.99

$9.99

You're the offense and use levers to move ball down field.. defense turns dial to stop you

Big Play Football
$6.99 without batteries

By selecting one of 14 levers, offense chooses from possible plays that occur in real NFL action. Defense counters with one of four proved NFL defenses. "Selectromatic Quarterback" records action. Scoreboard lights up to show whether offense or defense made the "Big Play." 28x15-in. hardboard playing surface. Metal frame. Uses 2 "D" batteries (order below).
79 N 304C—Shipping weight 6 lbs.. $6.99
"D" Battery. Shipping weight each 4 oz.
79 N 4660........ Each 16c; 4 for 60c

$5.33

Electric Pro Football
played on 29x15-inch gridiron

A flick of the switch and 2 teams of 3-dimensional players go into action. Dual-action kicker-passer throws forward passes and boots field goals. Metal grandstand, hardboard field. Also 2 scoring devices, goal posts, magnetic ball, yardage marker. Steel frame. Instruction booklet included. UL listed, 110-120-v., 60-c., AC.
79 N 104C—Shipping wt. 7 lbs..... $5.33

Crowd fills 3 sides of double-deck stands
Players run, block, tackle, receive passes in NFL Big Bowl Electric Football

$11.99

Surging excitement of a big crowd in a double-deck grandstand, only from Sears. Just set up your formations and watch 3-dimensional players clash on 36x21-inch field. Vibrating coil in field keeps men in action. Spectacular kicker-passer throws and boots magnetic ball. 3-man yardage marker and scoreboards keep track of the action. Set includes pennants, goal posts, 3 magnetic footballs, instructions and NFL plays. Paints and brush for painting players. Steel frame, plastic corners. Cord, coil operate on 110-120 volt, 60-cycle AC. UL listed. Partly assembled.
79 N 296L—Shipping weight 13 pounds.................$11.99

44 players paint them make 4 team

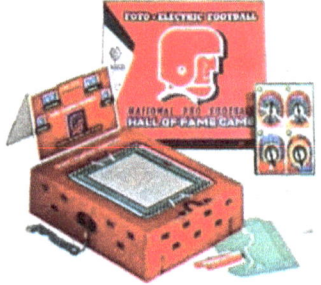

Foto-electric Football
$5.99

Quarterback your own team. Lighted gridiron shows plays in motion.. the action, suspense of pro games. "Hall of Fame" set includes offensive and defensive play cards, dials for kicks and runs, scoreboard. Laminated cardboard. UL listed, 110-120-v., 60-c. AC.
49 N 114C—Wt. 5 lbs.. $5.99

$5.99

Electro-magnetic Baseball
push buttons to pitch, bat

Touch of button delivers complete variety of "pitcher's specials." Arm powered by electronic coil. Second player presses a button and lever-action bat slams magnetic ball into play. 9 stationary metal players, scoreboard. Hardboard base 19x19 in., steel frame. UL listed, 110-120-v., 60-c. AC. Wt. 6 lbs.
79 N 418C............$5.99

442 SEARS 2L

1965 Montgomery Ward

CLASSIC ELECTRIC FOOTBALL $11.66

[A] $5.44 Electric Football Game
- Speed control
- Paint your own players

[B]
- Large 3-ft. gridiron
- Larger players in 5 realistic poses
- Offensive and defensive players can run, block, tackle
- Triple threat quarterback for each team can run, kick, pass
- Paint your own players; press on numerals
- Automatic timer stops and starts with each play
- Colorful grandstand with adjustable scoreboard

[A] ELECTRIC FOOTBALL GAME .. Two full teams, action posed 3-D players—linemen and backs. Quarterbacks run, pass, kick and even fumble. Water soluble paints to color players; press on numerals. Automatic timer; scoreboard; movable goal posts. Magnetic down markers. Improved speed control. Abt. 26x15½x1¾ in.
48 T 933 M—*Mailable*. Ship. wt. 4 lbs. $5.44

[B] CLASSIC ELECTRIC FOOTBALL GAME. Deluxe features include automatic timer that starts and stops with each play, and exclusive game board mountings which eliminate "dead spots" for continuous action. 24 large figures in 3-D action poses. Colorful grandstand crowd. Magnetic down and ball marker with chain. Colorful scoreboard. Move goal posts to college or pro positions. Speed control improved with printed dial and plastic knob. Four color palette of water soluble paints for coloring the uniforms in your own team colors. About 37¼x20¼x3 inches. *Mailable*.
48 T 934 MO—Ship. wt. 10 lbs. 12 oz. . . . $11.66

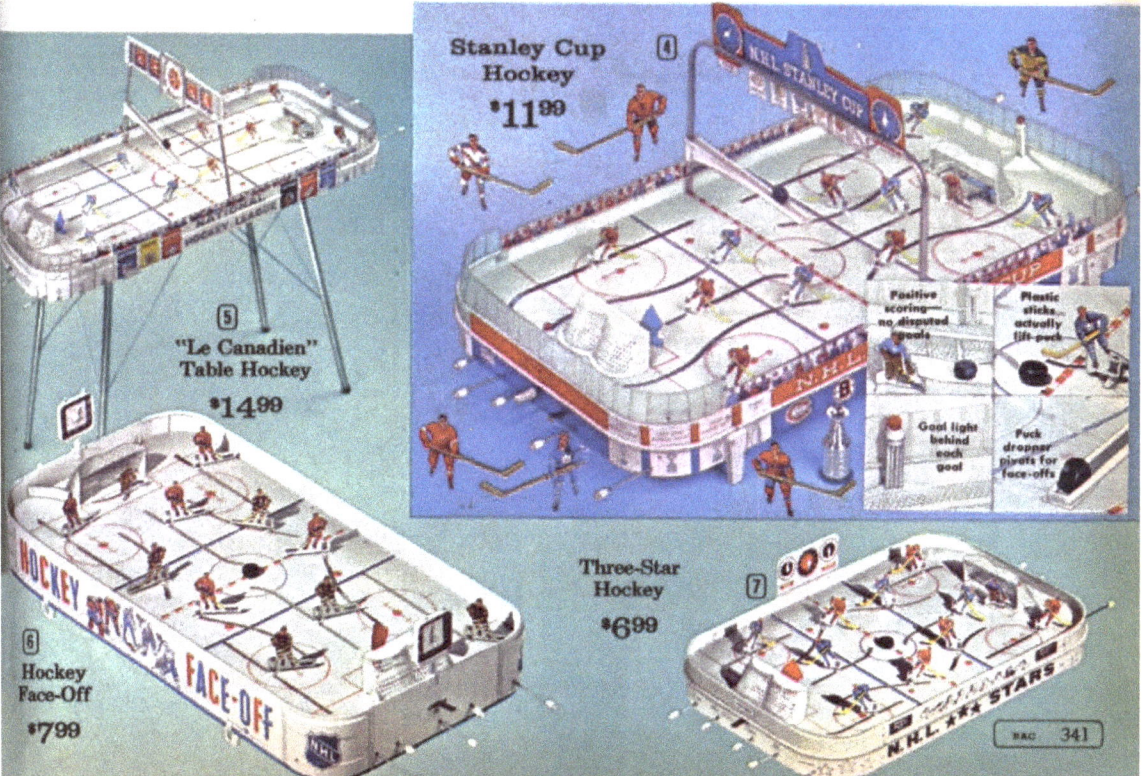

[4] Stanley Cup Hockey $11.99

[5] "Le Canadien" Table Hockey $14.99

[6] Hockey Face-Off $7.99

[7] Three-Star Hockey $6.99

- Positive scoring—no disputed goals
- Plastic sticks actually lift puck
- Goal light behind each goal
- Puck dropper pivots for face-offs

17

1966 Sears

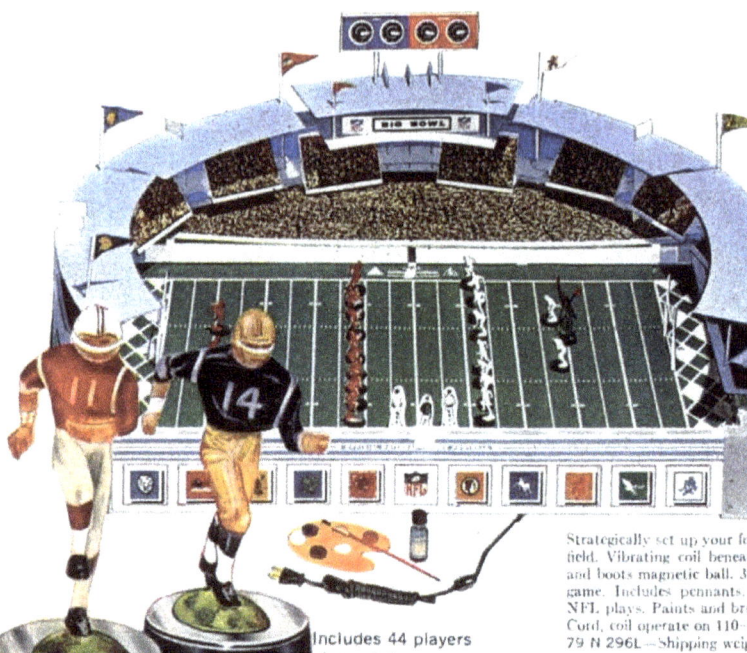

A capacity crowd fills the big double-deck stands..

Players run, pass and receive the ball as defensive team blocks and tackles..

NFL Big Bowl Electric Football Game

EXCLUSIVELY AT SEARS $11.99

Includes 44 players plus paints so you can make 4 different teams

Strategically set up your formations, then watch 3-D players clash on 36x21-in. field. Vibrating coil beneath keeps your men in action. Kicker-passer throws and boots magnetic ball. 3-man yardage marker and scoreboards keep track of game. Includes pennants, goal posts, 3 magnetic footballs, instructions and NFL plays. Paints and brush for painting players. Steel frame, plastic corners. Cord, coil operate on 110-120-v., 60-cycle AC. UL listed. Partly assembled.
79 N 296L—Shipping weight 12 pounds............ $11.99

Hitters actually run the bases
PRO LEAGUE BASEBALL
Swing the bat at a pitched ball, crank runners around to score

$9.99

A quick hand for turning gets men safely around bases in this multi-action version of pro-league baseball. Adjustable pitch control increases the excitement by delivering a complete variety of hard-to-hit pitches. Just a finger controls spring-action bat so game can be played alone or with opponent. Includes 9 stationary defensive players, multicolored grandstand, 4 removable base runners, steel baseball and 4-dial scoreboard. 22x22-in. plastic and hardboard base, steel frame. Buy it the easy way—order by phone.
79 N 120L—Shipping weight 10 pounds............ $9.99

$9.99

NFL Electric Football.. 36x21-in. gridiron

2 full teams of 3-D players plus a separate kicker-passer meet on vibrating gridiron. 2 magnetic footballs, 3-man yardage marker, goal posts, plays and instructions. Steel-framed hardboard. UL listed, 110-120-v., 60-c. AC. Shipping weight 12 pounds.
79 N 301L............$9.99

$5.99

Electric Pro Football on 29x15-in. gridiron

Flick switch and 2 teams of 3-D players plus kicker-passer move to action. Hardboard field, 2 scoring devices, goal posts, magnetic ball, yardage marker. Steel frame. UL listed, 110-120-v., 60-c. AC.
79N104C–Wt. 6 lbs.$5.99

$6.99

Foto-Electric Football

Lighted gridiron shows plays in action as you quarterback your team. "Hall of Fame" game includes offensive and defensive plays, dials for kicks and runs, scoreboard. Laminated cardboard. UL listed, 110-120-v., 60-c. AC. Shipping weight 5 pounds.
79 N 114C............$6.99

Arnold Palmer $5.89 Table Golf

Mechanical club hits ball down fairway, past hazards to felt green. Set your own hazards as skill increases. 19½x10½ in. wide. 2 "clubs", 8 plastic hazards, 3 rubber balls. Wt. 4 lbs.
79 N 130C......$5.89

1966 Montgomery Ward

1967 Sears

ELECTRIC FOOTBALL

Set up your formations .. players block, tackle, pass and receive. You control direction players move by turning each slightly to the left or right. Vibrating coil under field keeps magnetic football in play, makes action different every time.

$12.66

A capacity crowd fills the stands! Set up your formations strategically, then watch 3-D players clash on big 21x36 inch field. Kicker-passer throws and boots magnetic ball, defensive team blocks and tackles. Vibrating coil beneath field keeps men in action.

Paint players in the colors of your favorite teams. Game includes 3-man yardage marker and scoreboard, colorful pennants, goal posts, 3 magnetic footballs, instructions. UL listed, 110-120-v., 60-c., AC. Plastic players. Metal unit. Partly assembled.
79 N 65218L—Shipping weight 12 pounds.... $12.66

Includes 44 players (4 teams) plus paints. Now you can have your own bowl games!

Electric Pro Football.. quarterback your team $6.99

Flick switch on 29x15-in. gridiron and 2 teams of 3-D players plus kicker-passer go into action. 2 scoring devices, magnetic ball, yardage marker. Steel and hardboard. UL listed, 110-120-v., 60-c., AC.
79 N 104C—Shipping wt. 6 lbs..... $6.99

Foto-electric Football with lighted gridiron $7.59

"Hall of Fame" game includes offensive and defensive plays, dials for kicks and runs, scoreboard. Lighted gridiron shows plays in action. Laminated cardboard. UL listed, 110-120-volt, 60-cycle, AC.
79 N 114C—Shipping wt. 5 lbs..... $7.59

NFL ELECTRIC FOOTBALL

32x18-inch vibrating gridiron. Game includes all key plays of NFL teams, two 3-D teams.

$9.99

Now you can put your Monday morning quarterbacking into practice, manage two NFL teams in official, numbered uniforms. Ends, tackles, guards, offensive and defensive backs are posed in 3-D, plus 2 quarterbacks that kick, pass, and run. All steel game board has automatic timer, grandstand with scoreboard, yard and down markers, 6 felt footballs. UL listed, 110-120-v., 60-c., AC.
79 N 6551L—Shipping weight 8 pounds.... $9.99

Arnold Palmer Table Golf $5.99

Mechanical club hits ball down fairway, past hazards to felt green. Set your own hazards as skill increases. 19½x10½-in. wide. 2 "clubs", 8 plastic hazards, 3 rubber balls. Fun to play alone or in competition.
79 N 130C—Wt. 4 lbs.. $5.99

Baseball.. batters swing at pitched ball, run bases $9.99

You crank the runners around to score. A quick hand for turning helps score a run. Adjustable pitch control increases excitement by delivering a variety of pitches. Just a finger controls spring-action bat so game can be played alone or with opponent. 22x22-in. plastic and hardboard base; steel frame. Complete with 9 stationary defensive players, 4 removable base runners.
79 N 120L—Shipping weight 7 pounds........ $9.99

1967 Montgomery Ward

Wards NFL electric football
WITH 3-FT. GRANDSTAND ... SCOREBOARD

12⁸⁸

You're part of a vast crowd cheering classic football. Set up your formations ... 3-D players go into action on vibrating field. Triple threat quarterbacks run, pass, kick ... offensive, defensive players run, block, tackle ... 24 players including passer-kicker.

Automatic timer, speed control. Magnetic down and ball marker with chain. New center-post goal posts in official "NFL gold." Team uniforms are hand-painted replicas of Cleveland Browns and New York Giants. Grandstand folds easily for storage. Game about 37¾x20¼x3 in. UL listed.
48 HT 14503 A—Wt. 11 lbs. 13 oz. **12.88**

See pg. 345 for shipping information.

Bas-Ket basketball
3⁹⁹

[1] Bas-Ket is real basketball in miniature! Fast, competitive action every minute. Players control shots from anywhere in the court with mechanical levers. Real play action for "cage" fans of all ages. Sturdy construction, tested steel mechanisms. Court, scoreboard and game ball. About 20x12 in.
48HT14610—Wt. 3 lbs. 10 oz. **3.99**

Super Bowl electric football
5⁸⁸

[2] Super Bowl electric football is full of excitement! Two full teams, action-posed 3-D players. Quarterbacks run, pass, kick, even fumble. Automatic timer, speed control. Magnetic down markers. Goals move to college or pro positions. Scoreboard, grandstand. About 26x15½ in. UL listed. Ship. wt. 4 lbs. 13 oz.
48 HT 14505 M **5.88**

Pee-Wee hockey
7⁹⁹

[3] The ice, the action is always great in this big rink. Players of 2 NHL teams pass, block and score as they whip puck up and down the ice for high-pitched excitement. Adjustable steel legs; plastic score tower. Abt. 27½x16¼ in. Ship. wt. 7 lbs. 13 oz.
48 HT 14608 M **7.99**

NHL Stanley Cup hockey
12⁴⁴

[4] Super size rink, about 36x19½ in. Fast, realistic action: puck dropper pivots, sticks lift puck, lights flash when goal is scored! Players (in authentic NHL uniforms) move along rink and play behind nets. Overhead scoreboard. Adjustable steel legs. Plated replica of Stanley Cup. Buy 2 "D" batteries, page 288.
48 HT 14609 A—Wt. 11 lbs. 6 oz. **12.44**

1968 Sears

With 4 teams you can have your own championship playoffs

The linemen block or tackle while the backfield plunges into the line, runs around end or passes the magnetic football. Vibrating coil underneath a big 36x21-inch field sets each team into motion up or down the gridiron

Big Bowl Electric Football
$12.99

A capacity crowd fills the stands! Set up formations strategically, then watch 3-D players clash on field. Kicker-passer boots, actually throws magnetic ball, defensive team tries to stop ball carrier. Different results on every play. Game includes 3-man yardage marker, scoreboard, pennants, goal posts, 3 magnetic footballs, instructions. Metal unit, partly assembled. UL listed, 110–120-v., 60-c. AC. Paint plastic players in the colors of your favorite teams. Paints included.
79 N 65218L — Shpg. wt. 13 lbs. ... $12.99

4 teams, 64 players, plus an assortment of paints included

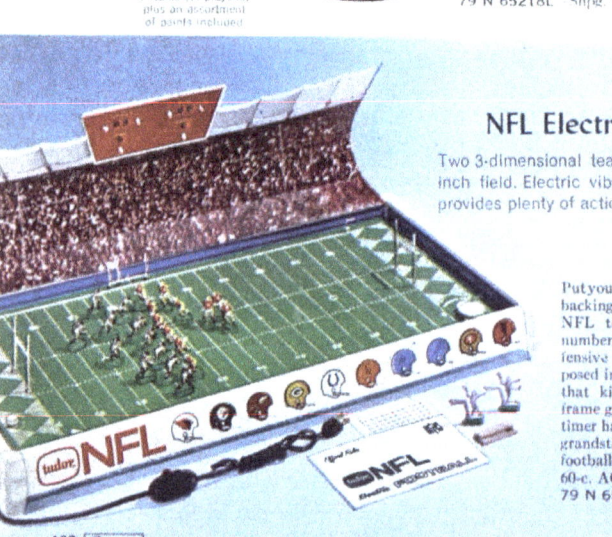

NFL Electric Football

Two 3-dimensional teams compete on 32x18-inch field. Electric vibrating coil underneath provides plenty of action.

$9.99

Put your Monday morning quarter-backing into practice .. manage 2 NFL teams in official, easy to number uniforms. Linemen and offensive and defensive backs are posed in 3-D, plus 2 quarterbacks that kick, pass and run. Steel-frame game board with automatic timer has yard and down markers, grandstand with scoreboard. 6 felt footballs. UL listed, 110–120-v., 60-c. AC. Shipping weight 9 lbs.
79 N 65019L $9.99

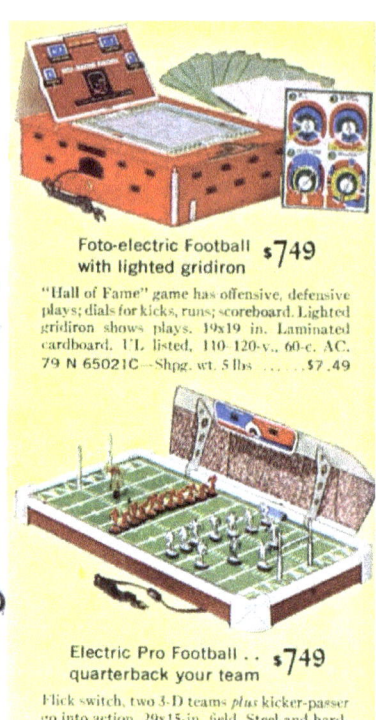

Foto-electric Football with lighted gridiron $7.49

"Hall of Fame" game has offensive, defensive plays; dials for kicks, runs; scoreboard. Lighted gridiron shows plays. 19x19 in. Laminated cardboard. UL listed, 110–120-v., 60-c. AC.
79 N 65021C — Shpg. wt. 5 lbs. $7.49

Electric Pro Football .. $7.49
quarterback your team

Flick switch, two 3-D teams *plus* kicker-passer go into action. 29x15-in. field. Steel and hardboard. Magnetic ball, scoring devices, marker. UL listed, 110–120-v., 60-c. AC.
79 N 65274C — Shpg. wt. 6 lbs. $7.49

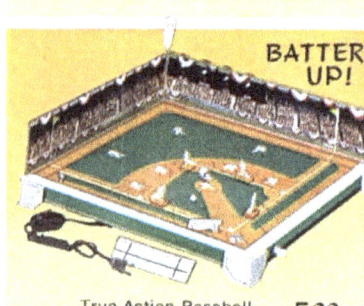

BATTER UP!

True Action Baseball .. $5.99
batter hits, runs bases

Bat connects with ball .. quick, flick switch and batter runs for first. Throwing device on center field wall tosses ball to the base to try to beat runner. Lever-action batting and pitching, 4 vibration-powered runners. 22x 22-inch steel-frame hardboard with score-board on fence. UL listed, 110–120-v., 60-c. AC.
79 N 65072C — Shpg. wt. 5 lbs. $5.99

Your strategy as manager $2.99
wins in All-Star Baseball

Make up your own all-star teams from 60 current American and National League players. Player discs show player's actual batting record, so each star bats exactly as he would in a regular game. Rules and scoring exactly as in pro ball. Managers spin dials, check results, employ special strategy. 19x12 in.
49 N 65155 — Shpg. wt. 2 lbs. $2.99

1968 Montgomery Ward

1968 Otasco (Generic Tudor Super Bowl)

1969 J.C. Penney

Penneys Year-Round **Sports Center**
Play all your favorite pro-type games indoors!

A 12.88 Super Dome electric football game

B 10.99 N.H.L. hockey game

C 2.88 N.H.L. Eastern League players

D 2.88 N.H.L. Western League players

E 14.44

F 5.99

G 5.88

1969 Sears

Super Bowl Electric Football
Jets and Colts clash head-on for the championship

Exclusively at Sears $14.99

- Jets are in official green and white . . Colts are in official blue and white
- Each team has a "quarterback" that passes, kicks, punts the ball
- Player identification numbers included
- Vibrating coil under board sets teams moving

Set up teams on field . . watch 'em tangle. The two champion AFL and NFL titans in 5 realistic poses meet on big 20x37-inch metal playing field. Every play's different! Kicker-passer actually throws or boots felt ball. Defensive team tries blocking ball-carrier. Automatic timer starts and stops with each play. Official Super Bowl field design. Set includes one-piece goal posts with realistic "protective" padding. Magnetic first-down marker with movable chain. Felt football. UL listed. 110–120-volt, 60-cycle AC.
79 C 6539L—Shipping weight 9 pounds.................$14.99

Super Dome Electric Football . . 21-inch high domed stadium.
Paint on your favorite team colors with paints included
$13.99

Action football strategy under realistic big dome. See 3-D teams clash in gridiron combat. One player on each team throws and kicks magnetic ball. Defense tries to stop opposing ball carrier. Hardboard 36x21-in. playing field and electric vibrator coil. Clear plastic and cardboard dome. Referee, yard marker, scoreboard, pennants, goal posts, 3 magnetic footballs. 4 teams, paints, instr. UL listed. 110–120-v., 60-c. AC.
79 C 65416L—Shpg. wt. 13 lbs.. . $13.99

NFL Electric Football with two 3-D teams
$11.99

Electric vibrating coil sends teams into action. Players compete on 32x18-inch metal field . . and are posed in easy-to-number NFL uniforms. Two quarterbacks kick, pass, fumble. Automatic timer; yard, down markers; grandstand and scoreboard. Six felt footballs. UL listed. 110–120-v., 60-c. AC.
79 C 65019L—Shipping weight 8 lbs........$11.99

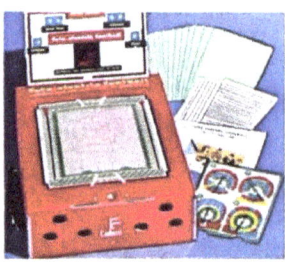

Foto-Electric Football has lighted gridiron $7.49

Offensive, defensive strategy is set on 19x19-inch game board. Play viewer is moved to reveal lighted field and results of running or passing plays. Spinner for kicking, runbacks, penalties. Paperboard. UL listed. 110–120-v., 60-c. AC.
79 C 65021C—Shpg. wt. 5 lbs.. . $7.49

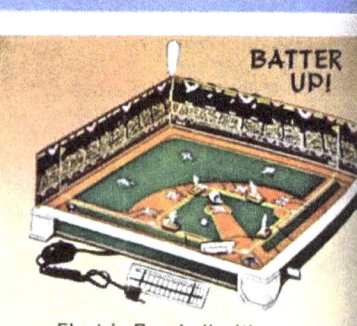

BATTER UP!

Electric Baseball with batters that hit and run $6.69

Hit ball . . batter "runs" for first. Throwing arm tosses ball trying to beat runner. Lever-action batting, pitching. Vibrator coil. Metal and hardboard, 22x22 inches. UL listed. 110–120-v., 60-c. AC.
79 C 65072C—Shipping weight 5 pounds......$6.69

For grandstand coaches.. All-Pro Baseball uses your baseball knowledge $4.79

Manage your own team. Utilize strategy and know-how of the sport with pitcher-batter selector. Big-league rules. Playing field, teams, dice, scoreboard.
79 C 65417C—Shipping weight 3 pounds......$4.79

1969 Montgomery Ward

Wards NFL electric football
with 3-ft. grandstand ... complete scoreboard **13.88**

3-D players give their all on the vibrating gridiron. Triple-threat quarterbacks run, pass, kick. Offensive-defensive players run, block and tackle. 24 players, including passer-kicker, wear the official team colors of the Cleveland Browns and the New York Giants.
Includes automatic timer and speed control. Magnetic down and ball marker with chain. Center-post goal posts in official "NFL Gold." All figures hand-painted for complete accuracy. Big grandstand, jammed with loyal fans, folds easily for storage. Game about 37¾x20¼x3 in. high. UL listed.
48 T 14510 A—Ship. wt. 11 lbs. 13 oz. **13.88**

Tru-Action electric football 6.99

Full of excitement! Game includes two full teams, 24 3-D players in all. Quarterbacks run, pass, kick, even fumble. Automatic timer, speed control. Magnetic down markers. Complete scoreboard. Paint your own teams with paint set included. About 26x15½ in. UL listed.
48 T 14505 M—Ship. wt. 4 lbs. 13 oz. **6.99**

NFL electric football 9.99

Thrilling electric football between the San Francisco 49ers and the Los Angeles Rams. The 24 players, including 2 passer-kickers, can do everything the real teams do except get injured. Automatic timer, speed control. Full scoreboard. About 31½x17½ in. UL listed.
48 T 14509 A—Ship. wt. 7 lbs. 6 oz. **9.99**

Bas-Ket 3.99

Enjoy real basketball in miniature with Bas-Ket. Full of excitement for "cage" fans of all ages. Fast, competitive action every minute! Players control shots from anywhere in the court with mechanical levers. Sturdy construction, tested steel mechanisms. Court, scoreboard, game ball included. Large playing court is about 20x12 in. wide.
48T14610—Wt. 3 lbs. 10 oz. **3.99**

Bowl 4.88

Hit the headpin, get a strike! Like real bowling, you'll need a good aim when you only have one pin left to make a spare. Hit the pins, they flip out of sight. Touch the lever and they all return to proper position. Ten 4½-in. plastic pins, bright lithographed metal housing, 3½-in. rubber ball. About 16x16x6 in. high.
48T14511—Ship. wt. 6 lbs. **4.88**

Major league electric baseball 6.97

Have endless fun-filled hours playing exciting electric baseball. Remote-controlled pitcher throws balls or strikes ... even change-ups to fool the batter. Control the batter to slam the magnetic ball for a homer, triple, double, single, even a bunt. Throw moving runners out at any base. Make double or triple plays.
Scoreboard keeps track of balls, strikes, outs, runs. Crowds fill grandstands. Includes 4 players, metal base, steel stand. For two players, ages 9 and up.
48 T 14514 M—110 volts, AC. UL listed. Ship. wt. 5 lbs. 2 oz. **6.97**

SAVE THIS CATALOG! Use it to order toys until August 31, 1970

1970 Sears

Vikings and Chiefs battle for the professional championship

Super Bowl Electric Football

Sold only at Sears $15.99

- Big 37x20-inch metal gridiron
- Both teams are in official colors
- Field decorations are exactly like the actual Super Bowl game
- Each team has a quarterback that passes, kicks, and carries the ball

Recreate the excitement of the biggest football game of the year as the AFL and NFL champions clash in the Super Bowl. Now you're the coach—you call the plays. Set up offensive and defensive formations. Vibrating coil under board sets players moving down the field. Colorful plastic "Vikings" and "Chiefs" are in five poses; players remove from bases for display. Set includes automatic timer, magnetic first-down marker with "chain," six felt footballs, one-piece goal posts. Colorful clip-on grandstand and scoreboard. Instructions and player identification numbers included. UL listed for 110–120-volt, 60-cycle AC.
79 N 65456L—Shipping weight 11 pounds..............$15.99

Packers and Rams clash on the field in NFL Electric Football

Teams wear official colors, and play on 32x18-inch metal field

$11.97

Two powerful NFL teams meet head-on. Colorful plastic players come in five action poses, vibrating coil sets them moving. Each team has a quarterback that throws, kicks and carries the ball. Set has automatic timer, movable magnetic down and yard markers. Goal posts, clip-on grandstand, 6 felt footballs. Instructions included. UL listed. 110–120-volt, 60-cycle AC.
79 N 65452C—Wt. 8 lbs......$11.97

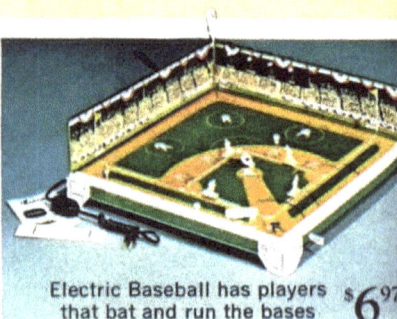

Electric Baseball has players that bat and run the bases $6.97

Hit ball.. plastic batter "runs" for first. Throwing arm tosses ball trying to beat runner. Lever-action batting, pitching. Vibrator coil. Metal and hardboard, 22x22 in. UL listed. 110–120-v., 60-c. AC.
79 N 65072C—Shipping weight 5 pounds......$6.97

NFL Electric Football with 27-inch gridiron $8.97

Action-posed plastic Jets and Raiders on metal field. Two quarterbacks pass, kick and carry ball. Includes automatic timer, magnetic down and yard markers, vibrating coil, clip-on grandstand, 6 felt footballs. 27x16 in. UL listed, 110–120-v., 60-c. AC.
79 N 65545C—Shipping weight 5 lbs......$8.97

Priced to be **SOMETHING SPECIAL** Was $7.49 $6.94

Cut 7%. Foto-Electric Football. Takes strategy. All new offensive and defensive plays.. move viewer for results. Spinner for kicking, runbacks, penalties. New design paperboard box, 19x14x4¾ in. Instr. UL listed, 110–120-v., 60-c. AC.
79 N 65021C—Shpg. wt. 5 lbs $6.94

You do the batting with Sure Shot Baseball $4.44

One player turns knob to hit ball.. the other tries to catch it as it pops over the outfield wall. Score the most runs in nine innings. Move plastic players around bases. Set includes 18x18-in. plastic play board, players, baseballs, instructions.
79 N 65544C—Shipping weight 3 pounds......$4.44

1970 Montgomery Ward

Wards NFL electric football
with 3 American and National Conference teams — $15.78

3-D players give their all on the vibrating gridiron. Triple-threat quarterbacks run, pass, kick. Offensive-defensive players run, block and tackle. 36 players, including passer-kicker, wear the official team colors of the Kansas City Chiefs, Cleveland Browns and Los Angeles Rams.

Includes automatic timer and speed control. Magnetic down and ball marker with chain. Center-post goal posts in official "NFL Gold." All figures handpainted for complete accuracy. Big 3 ft. grandstand, jammed with loyal fans, folds easily for storage. Game about 37¾x20¼x3 in. high. UL listed. Wards Exclusive!
48 T 14519 A—Ship. wt. 11 lbs. 13 oz. 15.78

Pro-star electric football — $10.79
action shot poster

Full of excitement! Game includes two full teams, 24 3-D players in all. Quarterbacks run, pass, kick, even tumble on vibrating field. Magnetic down markers and footballs. Complete grandstand, scoreboard. Licensed by Professional Football Players Assoc. 14x27 in. poster includes 42 action shots.
48 T 14523 M—Ship. wt. 9 lbs. 10 oz. Abt. 33x17 in. UL listed. 10.79

Bas-Ket — $4.69

Enjoy real basketball in miniature with Bas-Ket. Full of excitement for "cage" fans of all ages. Fast, competitive action every minute! Players control shots from anywhere in the court with mechanical levers. Sturdy construction, tested steel mechanisms. Court, scoreboard, game ball included. Large playing court is about 20x12 in. Wt. 3 lbs. 10 oz.
48 T 14610 ..... 4.69

NFL electric football — $12.49

Thrilling electric football between the Dallas Cowboys and the New York Jets. The 24 players, including 2 passer-kickers, can do everything the real teams do except get injured. Automatic timer, speed control. Full scoreboard. About 31½x17½ in. UL listed.
48 T 14521 M—Ship. wt. 7 lbs. 6 oz. 12.49

Electric baseball — $7.79

Official American and National League game. Remote-controlled pitcher throws balls or strikes ... even change-ups to fool the batter. Control the batter to slam the magnetic ball for a homer, triple, double, single, even a bunt. Throw moving runners out at any base. Make double or triple plays.

Scoreboard keeps track of balls, strikes, outs, runs. Crowds fill grandstands. 4 players, metal base, steel stand. 2 players, ages 9-up.
48 T 14514 M—110 volts, AC. UL listed. Ship. wt. 5 lbs. 2 oz. 7.79

Skittle pool — $12.49

FABULOUS VALUE

Play pool with a different "twist." Ball suspends on chain from metal arch. Swing ball at correct angle to hit cue ball into other balls to make your shot. This relaxing variation of pool appeals to all. Felt surface table, ball return, 10 numbered balls, cue ball, metal arch, swinging ball and chain, magic cue, ball rack, scoring counter. 23½x23¼x3¾ in. Wt. 11 lbs. 13 oz.
48 T 14879 A 12.49

1970 J.C. Penney

Penneys Year-Round **SPORTS CENTER**

Play all your favorite pro-type games indoors!

[A] 13.88 Super Dome electric football

Games that operate like computers

[C] 19.88

[B] 34.95

[D] 6.99

[E] 6.99

[F] 6.99

1970 Aldens

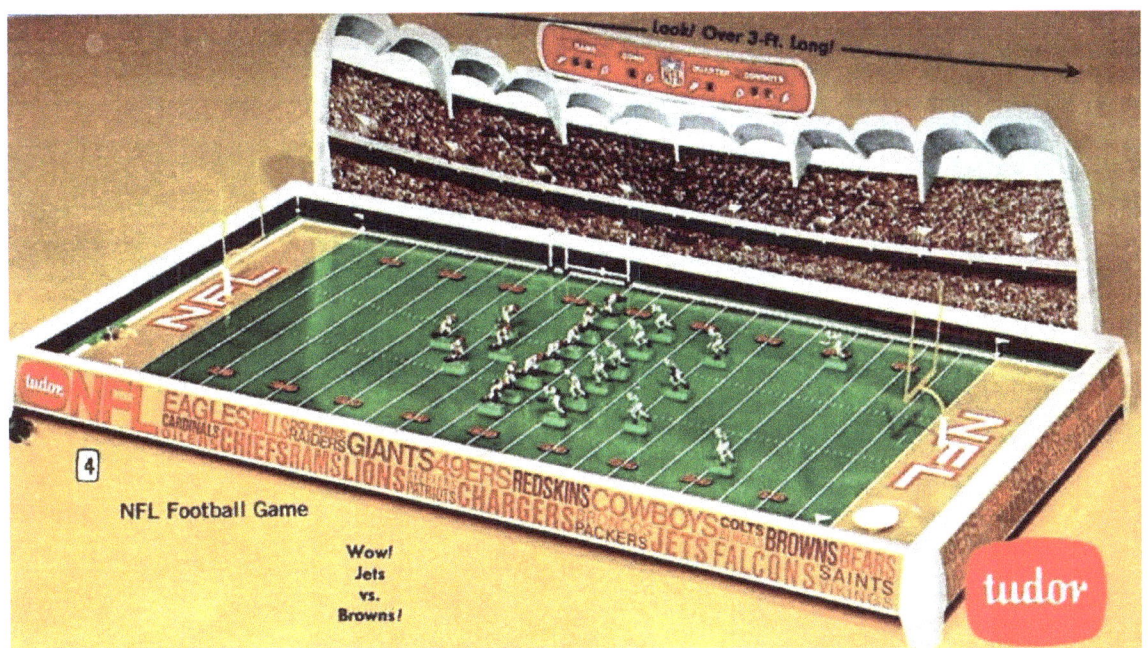

NFL Football Game

Wow! Jets vs. Browns!

Computer Football

Pro-Bowl 3-D Football Game! Giant 4 x 8-Ft. Field!

**Tudor NFL Electric Football Game
Brings Hours of Realistic Action** 13.88

4 Jets vs. Browns on giant 37¾x20¼x3-in. playing field. Watch the quarterbacks pass, kick, run with miniature football. Automatic timer, working scoreboard. Metal board.
E85 Y 7417E—115V, AC, UL. Wt. 10 lb. Mail./Exp........13.88
85 Y 7418E—Smaller 26½x15½x1¾" game. Wt. 6 lb. Mail. 7.77
85 Y 7421E—Giants vs. Bears. 31½x17½". Wt. 9 lb. Mail..12.95

**New from Computer Games...
Computer Football Game** 18.88

5 From the world of computer technology comes a new game for 2. Plan football strategy . . . the computer gives the results.
85 Y 7441E—Wt. 8 lb. Mail.......18.88

**Marx Pro-Bowl 3-Dimensional
Football Game—Giant 4x8-Ft. Field!** 10.97

6 Really big game. Plus lots of live action as simple or strategically complex as you desire. Mechanical runner.
85 Y 7420E—Shipping weight 7 lb. Mailable............10.97

**Gotham Official Joe Namath
Electric Football Game** 9.97

7 Magnetic football starring Joe. Watch him pass the ball to 22 live action players. Realistic 3D grandstand scoring device.
85 Y 7419E—Size: 36x20x15". Ship. wt. 8 lb. Mail. 115V, AC. 9.97

1971 Sears

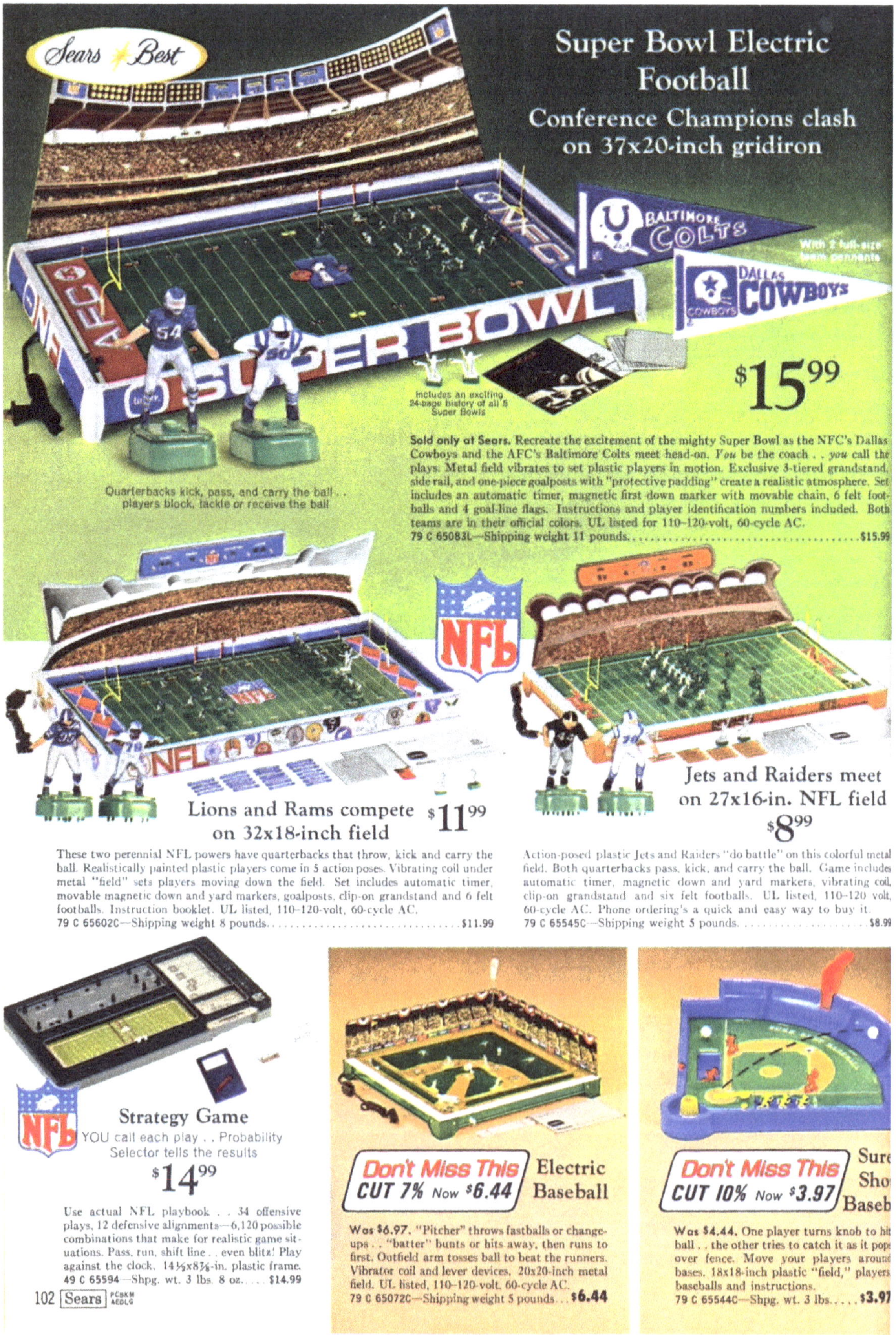

Super Bowl Electric Football
Conference Champions clash on 37x20-inch gridiron

$15.99

With 2 full-size team pennants

Includes an exciting 24-page history of all 5 Super Bowls

Quarterbacks kick, pass, and carry the ball.. players block, tackle or receive the ball.

Sold only at Sears. Recreate the excitement of the mighty Super Bowl as the NFC's Dallas Cowboys and the AFC's Baltimore Colts meet head-on. *You* be the coach .. *you* call the plays. Metal field vibrates to set plastic players in motion. Exclusive 3-tiered grandstand, side rail, and one-piece goalposts with "protective padding" create a realistic atmosphere. Set includes an automatic timer, magnetic first-down marker with movable chain, 6 felt footballs and 4 goal-line flags. Instructions and player identification numbers included. Both teams are in their official colors. UL listed for 110-120-volt, 60-cycle AC.
79 C 65083L—Shipping weight 11 pounds....................$15.99

Lions and Rams compete on 32x18-inch field
$11.99

These two perennial NFL powers have quarterbacks that throw, kick and carry the ball. Realistically painted plastic players come in 5 action poses. Vibrating coil under metal "field" sets players moving down the field. Set includes automatic timer, movable magnetic down and yard markers, goalposts, clip-on grandstand and 6 felt footballs. Instruction booklet. UL listed, 110-120-volt, 60-cycle AC.
79 C 65602C—Shipping weight 8 pounds.............$11.99

Jets and Raiders meet on 27x16-in. NFL field
$8.99

Action-posed plastic Jets and Raiders "do battle" on this colorful metal field. Both quarterbacks pass, kick, and carry the ball. Game includes automatic timer, magnetic down and yard markers, vibrating coil, clip-on grandstand and six felt footballs. UL listed, 110-120 volt, 60-cycle AC. Phone ordering's a quick and easy way to buy it.
79 C 65545C—Shipping weight 5 pounds................$8.99

Strategy Game
YOU call each play .. Probability Selector tells the results
$14.99

Use actual NFL playbook .. 34 offensive plays, 12 defensive alignments—6,120 possible combinations that make for realistic game situations. Pass, run, shift line .. even blitz! Play against the clock. 14½x8⅜-in. plastic frame.
49 C 65594—Shpg. wt. 3 lbs. 8 oz...... $14.99

Don't Miss This CUT 7% Now $6.44 Electric Baseball

Was $6.97. "Pitcher" throws fastballs or change-ups .. "batter" bunts or hits away, then runs to first. Outfield arm tosses ball to beat the runners. Vibrator coil and lever devices. 20x20-inch metal field. UL listed, 110-120-volt, 60-cycle AC.
79 C 65072C—Shipping weight 5 pounds... **$6.44**

Don't Miss This CUT 10% Now $3.97 Sure Shot Baseball

Was $4.44. One player turns knob to hit ball .. the other tries to catch it as it pops over fence. Move your players around bases. 18x18-inch plastic "field," players, baseballs and instructions.
79 C 65544C—Shpg. wt. 3 lbs..... **$3.97**

1971 Montgomery Ward

NFL Electric Football
Wards exclusive...
thoroughly lab tested

- 3 American and National Conference teams
- Deluxe grandstand and working scoreboard
- Deluxe league standings
- 26-team side panel
- NFL playbook

14.99

3-D players give their all on the vibrating gridiron. Offensive-defensive players run, block and tackle. 3 full teams wear the official team colors of the Baltimore Colts, Minnesota Vikings, San Francisco 49'ers. Plus 3 running, passing, kicking quarterbacks for 36 players in all. Automatic timer and speed control. Magnetic down and ball marker with chain. Goal posts in official "NFL Gold." Figures hand-painted in official NFL uniforms. 37¾x20¼ in. Heavy duty switch, safety plug. UL listed.
48 T 14527 A—Ship. wt. 11 lbs. 13 oz........ 14.99

NFL electric football 8.97

Dallas Cowboys take on the New York Jets in a key contest! 24 3-D players fight to win. Set your own plays. Quarterbacks run, pass, kick, even fumble on vibrating field. Magnetic 10-yd. marker with moveable chain. Timer, speed control. Grandstand. Hand painted players in official uniforms. 4 goal line flags. Heavy duty switch and safety plug. UL listed. About 26½x15½x1¾ in.
48 T 14529 M—Shipping weight 5 lbs. 11 oz................ 8.97

6.97 Electric baseball

Throw moving runners out at any base. Control the batter to slam the magnetic ball for homer, triple, double, single, even a bunt. Remote-controlled pitcher throws balls or strikes ... even change-ups to fool the batter. Make double or triple plays. Crowds fill grandstands. Full scoreboard. Scorecards. 4 players, metal base, steel stand. 110 volts, AC. UL listed. Ship. wt. 5 lbs. 2 oz.
48 T 14531 M.......... 6.97

NFL electric football 10.88

Chicago Bears vs. Kansas City Chiefs! Maneuver the 24 3-D players, including 2 passing, kicking, running quarterbacks to make the winning plays. Automatic timer, speed control. Full grandstand, scoreboard. Magnetic 10-yd. marker with moveable chain. 4 flags. "NFL Gold" posts. Handpainted figures. 31½x17½ in.
48 T 14528 M—Heavy duty switch, safety plug, UL listed. Wt. 7 lbs. 6 oz...... 10.88

New! Match Point Tennis 4.79

Serve, smash and return as actual tennis. You control the action. Rackets play close to the net while mechanical levers play the backcourt. Player controls his serve and returns from anywhere on the court. Ball may be hit high or low, left or right. Use strategy for lobs, smashes, and placements. Scoreboard, ball, net, 2 defending rackets, court.
48 T 14608—12½x20½x2¾ in. Ship. wt. 3 lbs. 14 oz............. 4.79

Skittle pool 11.99

FABULOUS VALUE

Check Wards low price! Play pool with a different "twist." Ball suspends on chain from metal arch. Swing ball at correct angle to hit cue ball into other balls to make your shot. Felt surface table, ball return, 10 numbered balls, cue ball, metal arch, swinging ball and chain, magic cue, ball rack, scoring counter. Abt. 23½x23¾x3¾ in. This relaxing variation of pool appeals to all ages. Ship. wt. 11 lbs. 6 oz.
48 T 14879 A.......... 11.99

BACKS 431

1971 Sears (Coleco)

Sports Table Games with legs .. set up almost anywhere

Hockey $24.95

Metal players pass, skate, and shoot for the goal as you push, pull, or twirl control rods. It's thrilling, high pressure hockey and you're right in the thick of the action. Automatic goal judge shows goals and end of periods. Puck ejector sends puck back into play after goals. Pull your goalie and add a sixth shotmaker for exciting "power-play" hockey. Overhead scoreboard shows score and league standings; side-mounted board shows penalty and game time. Handsome metal table has tubular steel legs, wood-grained panels. 38½x22x30-in. high. Canada.
6 C 25875N – Shipping weight 18 pounds.................$24.95

Extra Players. Hockey is even more fun when you have league competition. Set includes 12 complete teams of metal players in brightly colored uniforms. Use with table above. Canada.
6 C 25876 – Shpg. wt. 2 lbs.........$4.99

Table Soccer $49.95

[1] **Extra-large Table Soccer** with 26x49-inch playing area. You'll enjoy lots of rapid-fire action as two determined soccer teams battle it out. It's easy to play .. just push, pull and twirl chrome-plated telescoping rods to make players kick or block the ball. Each team has 11 plastic players 4¼ inches tall. Hardwood table stands 32 inches high. Full size wooden goal area. Metal legs keep table steady. Partially assembled. From Italy.
6 C 25886N – Shipping weight 32 pounds.................$49.95

[2] **Standard-size Table Soccer** is 18½x34-inch overall. Just twirl chrome-plated telescoping rods to make players kick or block the ball. Plastic players measure 3½ inches tall. Wooden table stands 28½ inches high. Folding metal legs.
6 C 25885L – Shipping weight 18 pounds.................$19.88

Thrill-packed Electric Football Game $29.95

Executive Command Control® lets you direct player movement **while plays are in progress!**

Magnetic control rods move players to give play flexibility and bruising realism not possible in conventional electric football games. You're in complete command as the play unfolds .. direct offensive and defensive running backs to run, block, tackle, and reverse. You direct the players of your choice. Attractive wood-grained finished metal; game 38x21x32 inches. Pro-style goal posts, yardage markers, end zone flags, and realistic scoreboard help recreate colorful atmosphere of a championship game. UL listed for 110-120-volt, 60-cycle AC. Panel style legs. Canada.
6 C 25878N – Shipping weight 17 pounds.................$29.95

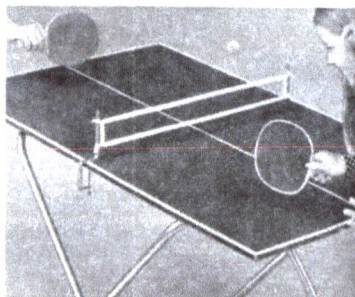

Mini Table Tennis Table

Great for today's modern apartments, or anywhere space is a problem

Table is a mere 2½x4½ ft., but you enjoy same kind of lively fun a full sized table gives. Bouncy, smooth ½-in. thick Plyblend® top gives great ball action. Collapsible 1-in. tubular steel legs adjust to 24 or 30 in. Green non-glare finish is pre-striped. Includes 2 balls, 2 paddles with pebbled rubber faces, net. Like everything else in Sears Books, it's so easy to order by telephone.
6 C 26045N – Shipping weight 30 lbs.........$19.77

NOTE: "N" items as (6 C 25875N) shipped by motor carrier or express.

1972 Spiegel

COMMAND CONTROL...
Electric football with remote control brings fast gridiron play!

15.88

You're the star quarterback in Coleco's exciting electric action football game. You and your opponent move 2 kicking, passing quarterbacks all about the gridiron... through the lines... right on down to "paydirt."
22 plastic players on vibrating field. 3-D metal grandstand and scoreboard. 38x21x3-in. 110-120V, AC. UL listed. Mail/Exp.
W36 J 3473—(14 lbs.)....15.88

PRO STAR ELECTRIC FOOTBALL by Coleco! 22 colorful "pros" move on electric vibrating gridiron in 3-D stadium (27x17x2 in.). 2 action quarterbacks make passing and kicking more realistic. Includes: Working metal scoreboard; magnetic footballs; yardage marker, corner flags; goal post. 110-120V, AC. UL listed.
Z36 J 3474—Mailable. Shipping weight 9 lbs.............9.95

ELECTRIC FOOTBALL GAME. Each team's plastic quarterback boots or passes ball... has eleven 3-D teammates! Move 'em into position... start the play! Goals move for pro or college game; magnetic markers, goal flags. Grandstand, scoreboard, automatic timer. Metal and plastic. 26½x15½x1¾ in. 110-120V, AC.
Z36 J 3308—UL listed. Mailable. Shpg. wt. 6 lbs..........6.95

SPORTS ILLUSTRATED PRO BASEBALL. Pit your ace pitcher against your foe's top batter in this play action baseball game based on official statistics of regular season play. Hit against left or right handed pitching. 24 color coded team charts with analysis of each major league team. 9x11-in field, 4 base runners.
35 J 3419—Shipping weight 3 lbs. 8 oz..................7.88

SPORTS ILLUSTRATED PRO FOOTBALL. Play the odds as you select the team most likely to win based on past performances. Has 9 plays, 6 defenses. 26 color coded team charts with analyses. Playing field with play selection dials; illustrated playbook; field position and down indicators; multi-dial scoreboard.
35 J 3407—Shipping weight 3 lbs. 8 oz..................7.88

See Page 285 for Spiegel Budget Power Terms—No Money Down

1972 Sears (Coleco)

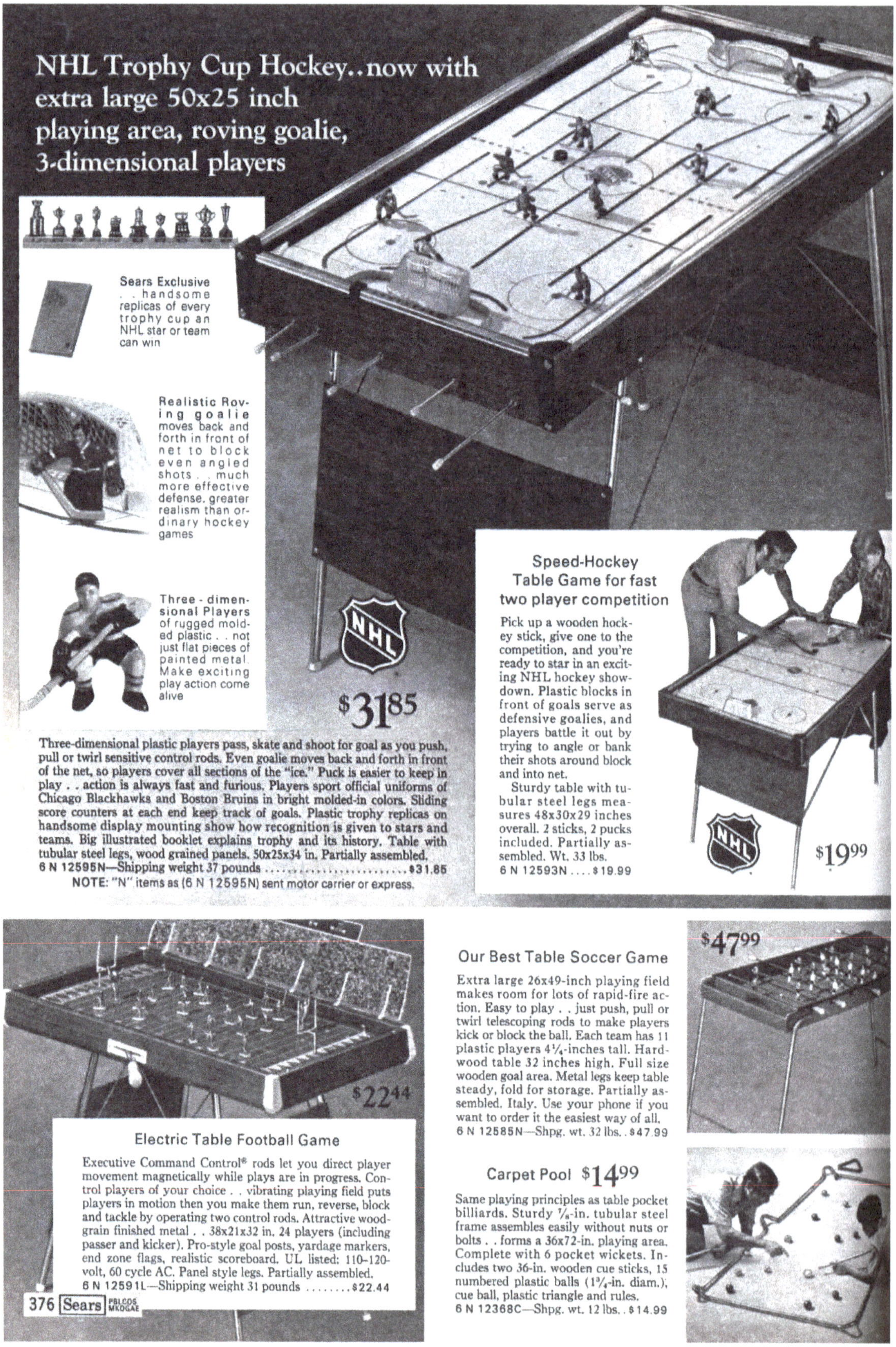

NHL Trophy Cup Hockey..now with extra large 50x25 inch playing area, roving goalie, 3-dimensional players

Sears Exclusive...handsome replicas of every trophy cup an NHL star or team can win

Realistic Roving goalie moves back and forth in front of net to block even angled shots...much more effective defense, greater realism than ordinary hockey games

Three-dimensional Players of rugged molded plastic...not just flat pieces of painted metal. Make exciting play action come alive

$31.85

Three-dimensional plastic players pass, skate and shoot for goal as you push, pull or twirl sensitive control rods. Even goalie moves back and forth in front of the net, so players cover all sections of the "ice." Puck is easier to keep in play..action is always fast and furious. Players sport official uniforms of Chicago Blackhawks and Boston Bruins in bright molded-in colors. Sliding score counters at each end keep track of goals. Plastic trophy replicas on handsome display mounting show how recognition is given to stars and teams. Big illustrated booklet explains trophy and its history. Table with tubular steel legs, wood grained panels. 50x25x34 in. Partially assembled.
6 N 12595N—Shipping weight 37 pounds $31.85
NOTE: "N" items as (6 N 12595N) sent motor carrier or express.

Speed-Hockey Table Game for fast two player competition

Pick up a wooden hockey stick, give one to the competition, and you're ready to star in an exciting NHL hockey showdown. Plastic blocks in front of goals serve as defensive goalies, and players battle it out by trying to angle or bank their shots around block and into net.

Sturdy table with tubular steel legs measures 48x30x29 inches overall. 2 sticks, 2 pucks included. Partially assembled. Wt. 33 lbs.
6 N 12593N $19.99

$19.99

Electric Table Football Game

$22.44

Executive Command Control® rods let you direct player movement magnetically while plays are in progress. Control players of your choice..vibrating playing field puts players in motion then you make them run, reverse, block and tackle by operating two control rods. Attractive woodgrain finished metal.. 38x21x32 in. 24 players (including passer and kicker). Pro-style goal posts, yardage markers, end zone flags, realistic scoreboard. UL listed: 110–120-volt, 60 cycle AC. Panel style legs. Partially assembled.
6 N 12591L—Shipping weight 31 pounds $22.44

Our Best Table Soccer Game $47.99

Extra large 26x49-inch playing field makes room for lots of rapid-fire action. Easy to play..just push, pull or twirl telescoping rods to make players kick or block the ball. Each team has 11 plastic players 4¼-inches tall. Hardwood table 32 inches high. Full size wooden goal area. Metal legs keep table steady, fold for storage. Partially assembled. Italy. Use your phone if you want to order it the easiest way of all.
6 N 12585N—Shpg. wt. 32 lbs.. $47.99

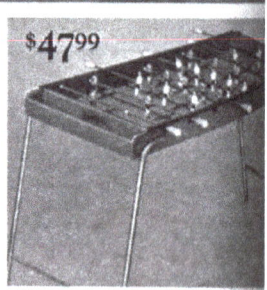

Carpet Pool $14.99

Same playing principles as table pocket billiards. Sturdy ⅞-in. tubular steel frame assembles easily without nuts or bolts.. forms a 36x72-in. playing area. Complete with 6 pocket wickets. Includes two 36-in. wooden cue sticks, 15 numbered plastic balls (1⅜-in. diam.), cue ball, plastic triangle and rules.
6 N 12368C—Shpg. wt. 12 lbs.. $14.99

1972 Sears (Munro)

1972 Sears

Now you control the play by programming each individual player to go forward, left or right!

NEW! TOTAL TEAM CONTROL

Steerable "legs" in the base of each player let *you* call the plays... secretly program your men "in the huddle"... then watch them slant or sweep right, left, or go straight up the middle!

Your quarterback's dropping back to pass...
but it's a fake! The halfback's coming around the end
The defensive line is fooled... can they react quickly enough?
Defensive backs charge to stop the ball carrier

SUPERBOWL Electric Football $15.99
SOLD ONLY AT SEARS

- Dolphins and Cowboys clash on 37x20-inch field
- Giant 1½x2-foot high Superbowl VI poster

This year Sears brings a whole new dimension to electric football! Now you can actually "tell" each player what pattern to run, what defender to block, how fast he should move.. to make the play go "all the way." You call each play by setting the adjustable "legs" on the players' bases for speed and direction. Then switch on the game and watch the vibrating metal field come alive. Includes 11 plastic players from each team molded in 5 realistic poses, 2 special quarterbacks that "run", "pass" or "kick", a 3-tiered grandstand backdrop, goal posts, automatic timer, first-down marker with movable chain, 6 felt footballs, 4 goal-line flags. UL listed for 110-120-v., 60-c. AC.
79 N 65614L—Shipping weight 11 pounds $15.99

Both sets include 2 "triple threat" Quarterbacks

NFL Electric Football $12.59
Lions and Rams compete on a 31½x17½-inch gridiron

Features the same exciting Total Team Control™ feature as the Superbowl set above. 22 players painted in the official colors of the Detroit Lions and the Los Angeles Rams "square off" on a colorful metal field. Vibrating coil beneath sets realistically posed players in action! Set includes automatic timer, movable magnetic down and yard markers, goal posts, clip-on grandstand, 6 felt footballs and an instruction booklet. UL listed, 110-120-volt, 60-cycle AC.
79 N 65695C—Shipping weight 9 pounds $12.59

Jets and Raiders collide on 27x16-in. NFL Electric Football $8.99

Action-posed plastic Jets and Raiders "do battle" on this colorful metal field. Both quarterbacks pass, kick and carry the ball.. vibrating coil moves ball-carrier. Automatic timer, magnetic down and yard markers, clip-on grandstand, 6 felt footballs. UL listed, 110-120-v., 60-c. AC. Phone ordering's a quick and easy way to buy it!
79 N 65545C—Shipping weight 5 pounds $8.99

Foto-Electric Football $6.99
The official game of the National Pro Football Hall of Fame
Slide in your preprinted offensive pattern.. opponent slides in defensive alignment.. lighted electric Play-Viewer measures your coaching ability! Spinner for kicking, runbacks, penalties. 19x14¾x4¾ in. UL listed.
79 N 65021C—110-120-v., 60-c. AC. Wt. 5 lbs. $6.99

AURORA MONDAY NIGHT FOOTBALL $8.99 without battery

Choose offense and defense.. push "Readout" button
Computerized football! Kickoff.. play over 280 plays. Instant-readout lights up yards gained (or lost) on field. 21x16x5 in. high. Uses 1 "AA" battery.. order pkg. at right.
79 N 65711C—Shipping weight 4 pounds $8.99

STRATEGY $15.35
The brain game for serious football nuts over 6000 play possibilities

Use an authentic NFL playbook.. 34 offensive plays, 12 defensive alignments.. to create realistic game situations. Pass, run, shift your line.. even blitz! Time-out and timer mechanisms allow you to play against the clock. 14½x8⅞-inch plastic frame.
49 N 65594—Shpg. wt. 4 lbs. $15.35

"AA" Batteries. (6). For game at left.
49 N 8402—Wt. 6 oz. ......Pkg. 99c

500 Sears

1972 Montgomery Ward

NFL Electric Football 14.99   NFL Electric Football 19.99

A You control EVERY player with TTC —Total Team Control! 3-D players give their all on the vibrating gridiron. Offensive-defensive players run, block and tackle. Dallas Cowboys vs. the Kansas City Chiefs! 2 full teams wear their official team colors. Automatic timer and speed control. Magnetic down and ball marker with chain. Handpainted team figures.

Wards Exclusive Electric football is thoroughly lab tested! Deluxe grandstand and working scoreboard keeps score of the exciting contest. League standings board, too. 26 NFL team side panel for a professional effect. Goal posts in official "NFL Gold." NFL playbook. 37¾x20¼ in. Heavy duty switch, safety plug. UL listed.
48 G 14552 A—Wt. 11 lbs. 13 oz..14.99

B WARDS EXCLUSIVE! NFL TABLE FOOTBALL! The Miami Dolphins take on the San Francisco 49'ers in a key contest! And most exciting of all, you control the action of EVERY player with Total Team Control! 24 3-D players fight to win. 4 officials referee the game. Players run, kick, even fumble on vibrating field. Magnetic 10-yd. marker with moveable chain.

Special scrimmage line separator... easy to set up plays. Deluxe league standings board. Thoroughly lab tested. Handpainted figures with official team colors. Automatic timer, speed control. Deluxe grandstand, working scoreboard. 26-team NFL side panel. NFL playbook. 37¾x20¼ in. Heavy duty switch, safety plug. UL listed.
48 G 14553 A—Wt. 14 lbs. 14 oz. 19.99

9.97   9.87

NEW! Talking Football   NEW! Soccer Game   NEW! Quarterback Game

C Sports announcer calls the play-by-play football game! It is tough gridiron competition as each player selects his team strategy! Offense chooses one of the recorded plays to move the ball down the field. Defense counteracts the quarterback's strategy. Then the spectators *hear* the action. Plays continue until a score! Records, rack, record player, spin-dial scoreboard, moving football, markers, goal posts. 1 "D" batt., order p. 240. Abt. 31x14 in.
48 G 14604 M—Ship. wt. 4 lbs. 3 oz.......... 9.97

D Dribble... then kick the ball down the field into good position! Fake the goalie... shoot! Goal! Table-top soccer game folds for easy portability and storage. Team figures are mounted on chrome plated, telescopic rods with plastic handles. Hardwood field with 12 players. 29½x17½x 2⅝ in. high when open. Recessed carrying handles. Instructions. From France. A soccer game the entire family will enjoy!
48 G 14672 M—Ship wt. 10 lbs. 13 oz......... 9.87

E ONLY AT WARDS! An unbelievable price for this unique "computerized" football game! Shop around and see for yourself! 12 seconds remaining in the game ... the bomb ... a field goal ... a halfback draw? You decide the strategy. Choose a card with the "best" offensive play ... wait for opponent to set up defense. Push "read out" button, result lights up. About 17x11 in. Needs two "AA" batteries, order on page 240.
48 G 14554—Wt. 2 lbs. 6 oz.,......5.66   ALL 281

1972 J.C. Penney

1972 J.C. Penney

1 to 3 Action Electric Football Games. Watch your team rush to victory as offensive and defensive players move across vibrating gridiron. Games include hardboard field with metal and plastic frame, grandstand, working scoreboard and two complete molded football teams with magnetic bases. Plug into any 110-120 volt, AC outlet. UL listed.

[1] Command Control Electric Football Game. You and your opponent each have complete magnetic control of one offensive or defensive back. Two action quarterbacks kick and pass. Includes automatic timer. Extra-large game field 38x21 in. Ages 7 to adult. Mailability restricted—see page 290. Shpg. wt. 11 lbs.
X 925-7940 A 16.44

Same as above, but with panel-style legs. Legs fold for storage and easy portability. 29 in. high overall. Mailability restricted—see page 290. Shpg. wt. 17 lbs.
X 923-8742 A 19.99

[2] Official NFL Electric Football. Players all in uniforms of two NFL teams. You can determine the direction of each player by setting the base control of each player before play begins. Field measures 31½x17½ in. Ages 7 to adult. Mail. wt. 8.25 lbs.
X 923-8759 A 9.99

[3] Pro Stars Electric Action Football. Action quarterback punts and passes. Action football for ages 7 to 12. Field measures 26x16 in. Mail. wt. 2.50 lbs.
X 923-8767 A 6.44

[4] Talking Football. Pick your own strategy, then hear the play in action. You pick a record for offensive play and opposition dials a defense, then listen to the play by play action broadcast over the "sportscaster". Winning depends on picking the right strategy. Plays were designed to challenge both experts and rookies. Includes one "D"-cell battery-operated "sportscaster" (battery not included, order below), 13 records and record rack, spin dial scoreboard, field markers, moving football and playing field with goal posts. Ages 6 to 12. Wt. 2.20 lbs.
X 923-8775 A 9.88

[5] Computer Sports Game. All the fun and excitement of football, basketball, hockey, soccer and baseball in one game. Offensive player pushes 2 activator buttons. Defensive player selects one of his—the computer figures the odds and errors that could occur and lights flash giving the results of the play immediately. Includes football field and two other reversible fields, so you can play all 5 games on one console. Wood and hardboard playing board, 17x22 in. For ages 9 to adult. Operates on 4 "AA"-cell batteries (included). Mail. wt. 7 lbs.
X 924-0474 A 19.88

[6] Computamatic football game. Offensive player secretly selects his choice of plays based on situation; defensive player uses his most effective defense against suspected offensive play. Choices increase or decrease chances of success. "Computer" immediately flashes results. Green and woodtone, plastic console, lighted plexiglass playboard is 22 in. x 17 in. To play hockey or basketball on console, order overlays below. Hardboard base. Uses 4 "AA"-cell batteries (included). Ages 9 to adult. Mail. wt. 7 lbs.
X 924-0102 A 34.95

Plastic overlays let you play your favorite sports on the console above by just slipping in the overlay.

Hockey Overlay. Mail. wt. 2 lbs.
X 923-8809 A 8.66

Basketball Overlay. Mail. wt. 2 lbs.
X 923-8817 A 8.66

"AA"-Cell Batteries. Pkg. of 4.
X 957-1902 A—0.40 lb. ...... 1 pkg. 69c

"D"-Cell Batteries. Pkg. of 6.
X 957-1761 A—1.40 lbs. ..... 1 pkg. 99c

CHARGE IT—see page 287

Table-height Electric Football

Table folds for portability and storage

Electric Football on folding legs. Hardboard playing surface allows exclusive magnetic ball action. Run, block, pass, tackle. Game plugs in, you flip a switch and 3-D players "go." Steel construction. Molded kicker/passer can even kick field goals. 2 full teams of molded players. Aluminum folding legs. Rounded plastic corners. 28¼x15¼x27 in. high. 110-120 volts AC. UL listed. Ages 8 to adult. Wt. 9 lbs.
X 925-7965 A 9.99

Computerized Monday Night Football
Over 280 different play possibilities. Each player secretly selects his play, then presses the "Read Out" button. You can see the results of the play flashed on the playing field immediately. Includes players, yard marker, goal posts and scoreboard. Black plastic console 21x16 in. wide, 5 in. high. Operates on one "AA"-cell battery (not included, order batteries at left, bottom of page). For ages 7 years old to adult.
X 923-8783 A—Mailing weight 4 lbs. 8.88

[9] Foto-Electric Football Game. Choose your offensive; your opponent sets his defense. Play-viewer actually shows ball carrier in motion until he's stopped. With field, scoreboard, 12 offensive and 8 defensive plays, kicking and run-back dials in full color. 19x15x4¾ in. high. 110-120 volts, AC. UL listed. For ages 10 years old to adult.
X 923-2562 A—Mailing weight 4.50 lbs. ... 6.99

Live-Action Football Game. Indoor football game with all the excitement of the real thing. Opposing players are lined up on a 3½x7 ft. printed vinyl field. Each side has a windup mechanical runner, quarterback-passer-kicker, and line backers on wheels. From kickoff to actual extra point kick, every play is possible—players move for you. Scoreboard, goal posts, tiny plastic footballs. For ages 7 years old to adult.
X 924-1191 A—Mail. wt. 9.20 lbs. 8.99

JCPenney 431

1973 Aldens

COLECO PRO SPORTS YOU'VE SEEN ON TV

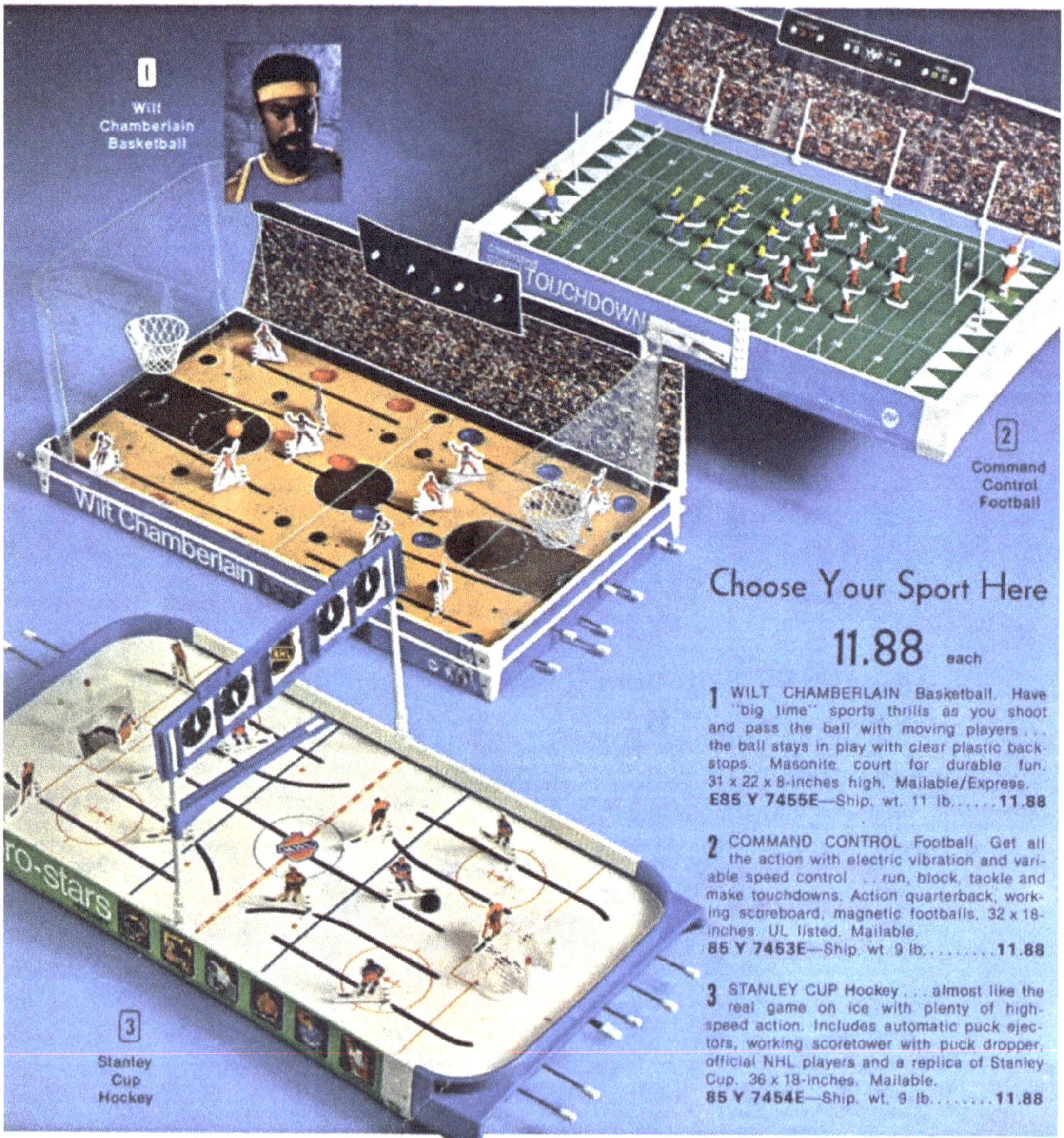

1 Wilt Chamberlain Basketball

2 Command Control Football

3 Stanley Cup Hockey

Choose Your Sport Here
11.88 each

1 WILT CHAMBERLAIN Basketball. Have "big time" sports thrills as you shoot and pass the ball with moving players... the ball stays in play with clear plastic backstops. Masonite court for durable fun. 31 x 22 x 8-inches high. Mailable/Express.
E85 Y 7455E—Ship. wt. 11 lb......**11.88**

2 COMMAND CONTROL Football. Get all the action with electric vibration and variable speed control... run, block, tackle and make touchdowns. Action quarterback, working scoreboard, magnetic footballs. 32 x 18-inches. UL listed. Mailable.
85 Y 7453E—Ship. wt. 9 lb........**11.88**

3 STANLEY CUP Hockey... almost like the real game on ice with plenty of high-speed action. Includes automatic puck ejectors, working scoretower with puck dropper, official NHL players and a replica of Stanley Cup. 36 x 18-inches. Mailable.
85 Y 7454E—Ship. wt. 9 lb........**11.88**

4 New!

Moto Cross Pinball

- the thrills of a motorcycle race
- the "real life" sound of an engine
- action wheels that keep on moving
- automatic speedometer to keep score

14.88

4 Battery-powered wheels keep ball in constant motion, making it crash into bell. Hand brakes make "varoom" sound. Plastic. 30 x 21-inches. Uses 2 "D" Cells, sold below.
85 Y 7456E—Ship. wt. 11 lb. Mailable. **14.88**
83 Y 3975—6 "D" Batteries 1 lb. 7 oz. **6/99c**

84 • ALDENS

1973 Sears (Munro)

1973 Montgomery Ward

Get your home team with Wards Exclusive NFL electric football

$19.99 with legs

[A] You're more than just a spectator... you're part of the action with Total Team Control—controlling every player to run, block and kick. You get your home team and opposing team—see below. 22 prepainted, 3-D players in 5 realistic poses add to real-life action. Automatic timer and speed control. Magnetic 1st down marker, goal posts, scrimmage line separator, 4 referees, play book. Grandstand with scoreboard. League standings board, too. Field about 37¾ in. long, 20¼ in. wide, 30 in. from floor. Heavy-duty switch, safety plug. UL listed.
48 T 14538 M—Ship. wt. 14 lbs. 19.99

If You Order from	You Get These Teams
Albany	Jets and Giants
Baltimore	Colts and Rams
Chicago	Bears and Vikings
Denver	Chargers and Raiders
Ft. Worth	Cowboys and Saints
Kansas City	Chiefs and Cardinals
Oakland	Raiders and Chargers
Portland	Raiders and Chargers
St. Paul	Vikings and Bears

Table-top model $14.87

[B] You get your home team plus all the exciting fun and action of NFL football game (A) above... no legs. 37¾x20¼ in.
48 T 14537 M—Ship. wt. 11 lbs. 14.87

Talking football $9.65

[C] Sports announcer calls the play-by-play action. It's tough gridiron competition as each player selects his team's strategy. 13 interchangeable records with 96 different plays. Offense chooses one of the recorded plays to move the ball down the field. Defense counteracts the quarterback's strategy. Then the spectators hear the action. Includes everything you need to see and hear real-life action—records, rack, record player, spin-dial scoreboard, moving football, markers, goal posts. Uses one "D" battery—order on page 308.
48 T 14604 M—About 31x15 in. Ship. wt. 3 lbs. 8 oz. 9.65

NEW! See-Action football $7.96

[D] Actually see the play develop with over 288 combinations! 28 slides—each player has 14 slides (8 offensive and 6 defense plays). Offensive quarterback picks his play, his opponent sets the defense. Then two slides are inserted into projector and you see the action. Random selector allows three possible outcomes for each combination of plays—you won't know outcome until last play appears on screen. Speciality plays (kick offs, punts, fumbles, returns and field goals) are determined by spinner. Includes projector, slides, playing board, scoreboard, goal posts, ball and first down markers, coin and spinner. Requires 4 "D" batteries—order on page 308.
48 T 14080—16¼x22¼x4½ in. Ship. wt. 3 lbs. 12 oz. 7.96

Monday-Nite football $8.86

[E] Over 1480 different play possibilities are fully computerized. Full of thrills and excitement right up to the last remaining seconds. After offensive and defensive plays are chosen, players push read-out button and instantaneous results light up on the playing field surface. Includes players, markers, goal posts and built-in scoreboard. Requires 2 "AA" batteries—order on page 308.
48 T 14536—About 21x5x16 in. Ship. wt. 4 lbs. 8.86

Budget electric football $8.99

[F] Official NFL football at a great low price. Whether it's running, blocking or tackling, you have total team control over all the Miami Dolphin and Green Bay Packer players. All 22 players are painted in official colors. Automatic timer and speed control adds to skill and excitement. Magnetic down and yard markers. Clip-on grandstand shows score, down and quarter. Heavy-duty switch, safety plug, UL listed.
48 T 14539 M—About 27x16 in. Ship. wt. 4 lbs. 8 oz. 8.99

1973 J.C. Penney

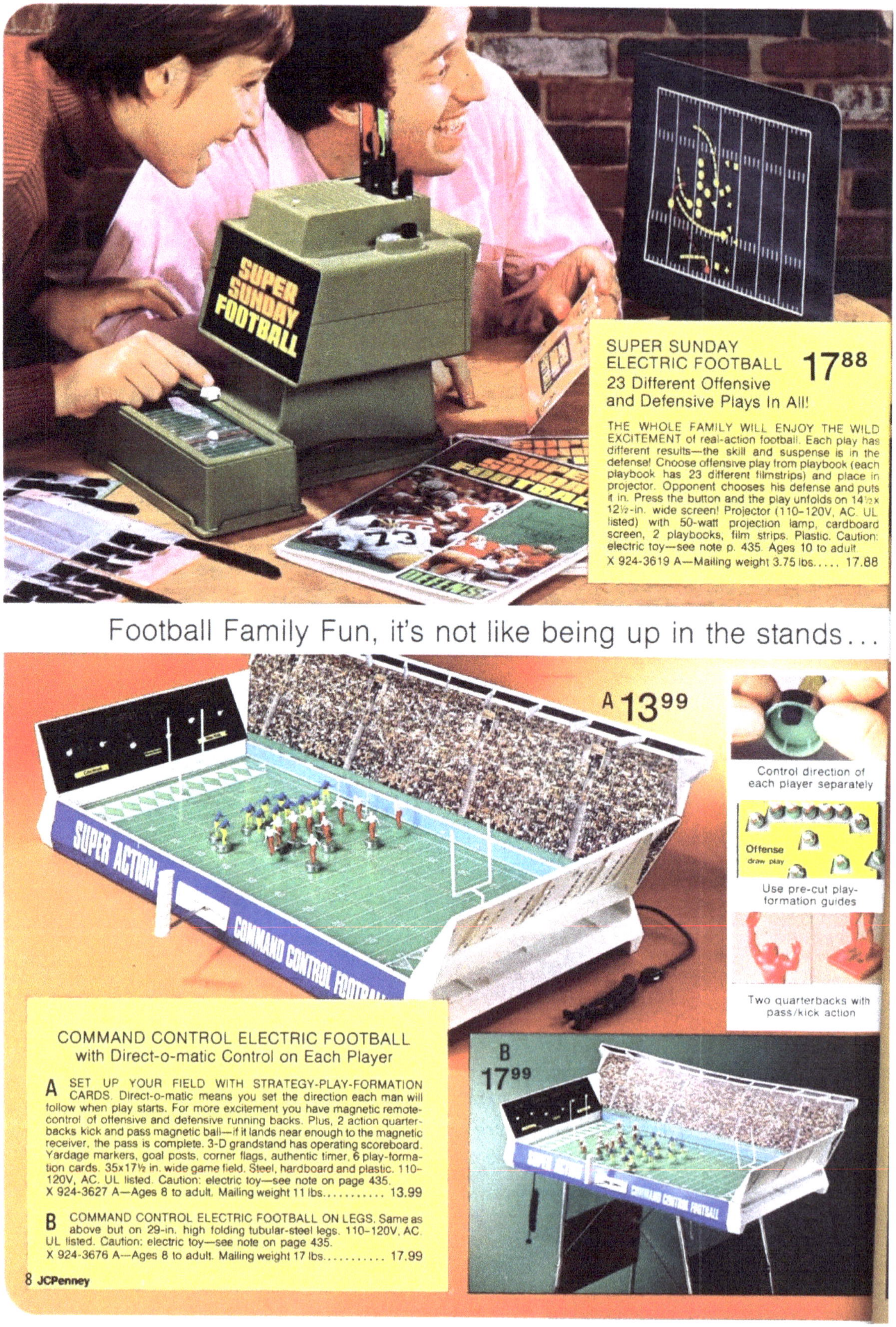

SUPER SUNDAY ELECTRIC FOOTBALL — **17.88**
23 Different Offensive and Defensive Plays In All!

THE WHOLE FAMILY WILL ENJOY THE WILD EXCITEMENT of real-action football. Each play has different results—the skill and suspense is in the defense! Choose offensive play from playbook (each playbook has 23 different filmstrips) and place in projector. Opponent chooses his defense and puts it in. Press the button and the play unfolds on 14½ x 12½-in. wide screen! Projector (110–120V, AC, UL listed) with 50-watt projection lamp, cardboard screen, 2 playbooks, film strips. Plastic. Caution: electric toy—see note p. 435. Ages 10 to adult.
X 924-3619 A—Mailing weight 3.75 lbs..... 17.88

Football Family Fun, it's not like being up in the stands...

A **13.99**

Control direction of each player separately

Offense draw play

Use pre-cut play-formation guides

Two quarterbacks with pass/kick action

B **17.99**

COMMAND CONTROL ELECTRIC FOOTBALL
with Direct-o-matic Control on Each Player

A SET UP YOUR FIELD WITH STRATEGY-PLAY-FORMATION CARDS. Direct-o-matic means you set the direction each man will follow when play starts. For more excitement you have magnetic remote-control of offensive and defensive running backs. Plus, 2 action quarterbacks kick and pass magnetic ball—if it lands near enough to the magnetic receiver, the pass is complete. 3-D grandstand has operating scoreboard. Yardage markers, goal posts, corner flags, authentic timer, 6 play-formation cards. 35x17½ in. wide game field. Steel, hardboard and plastic. 110–120V, AC. UL listed. Caution: electric toy—see note on page 435.
X 924-3627 A—Ages 8 to adult. Mailing weight 11 lbs.......... 13.99

B COMMAND CONTROL ELECTRIC FOOTBALL ON LEGS. Same as above but on 29-in. high folding tubular-steel legs. 110–120V, AC. UL listed. Caution: electric toy—see note on page 435.
X 924-3676 A—Ages 8 to adult. Mailing weight 17 lbs.......... 17.99

8 JCPenney

1973 J.C. Penney

SEE-ACTION FOOTBALL lets you watch plays come to life on the screen! **9.99**

YOU CALL THE PLAY, OPPONENT SETS DEFENSE—THE WHOLE FAMILY WATCHES THE RESULTS! Over 250 plays from 28 slides —14 for each team. Project plays onto screen. But you're never sure of the outcome! Random selector-switch on projector allows 3 possible results—one appears on screen. Record the play action on playing field, game statistics on scoreboard. Projector uses 4 "D" batteries (not incl., order below). Spinner (for special plays); coin; goals; ball; down markers. Plastic. 16x15x10¼ in. high.
X 924-3841 A—Ages 7 to adult. Mailing weight 4 lbs........ 9.99
X 957-1761 A—Pkg. 6 "D" batteries 1.40 lbs.........Pkg. 1.19

...it's like being on the field!

A **10.99**

Control direction of each player separately

2 triple-threat quarterbacks— run, pass, kick

B **9.99**

One quarterback with kicking/passing action

TOTAL-TEAM-CONTROL ELECTRIC FOOTBALL

A EXCITING NFL-STYLE ACTION BECAUSE YOU SET THE DIRECTION OF EACH PLAYER SEPARATELY! Triple-threat quarterbacks kick, pass, run too! Players in 5 realistic poses. Working scoreboard. Automatic timer starts/stops with each play. First-down marker with moveable 10-yd. chain. Magnetic ball; goal posts and flags; speed control; on/off switch. 31½x17½ in. wide field. Steel, hardboard, plastic. 110–120V, AC. UL listed. Caution: electric toy—see note on page 435. Ages 8 to adult.
X 923-8759 A—Mailing weight 8.25 lbs....................10.99

B ELECTRIC FOOTBALL WITH FOLDING TUBULAR-ALUMINUM LEGS. Flip the switch and watch 3-D players go! Kicking/passing quarterback even kicks field goals. Magnetic ball, goal posts, on/off switch. 28¼x15¼x27 in. high. Steel, hardboard, plastic. 110–120V, AC. UL listed. Caution: electric toy—see note on page 435. Ages 8 to adult.
X 925-7965 A—Mailing weight 9 lbs.....................9.99

SAVE THIS CATALOG—order anything on these two pages till August 24, 1974

1974 Sears

You're the head coach with these Electric Football Games

- This wheel in each player's base offers Total Team Control. Program their "legs" to run sweeps, slants or up the middle.
- Triple-threat quarterback on each team can run, pass or even kick.

Only at Sears! SUPERBOWL
Dolphins and Vikings clash on a 31½x17½-inch gridiron **$14.94**

1. Total Team Control lets you "tell" each player what pattern to run, what defender to block, to make the play "go all the way." Switch on the game and watch the vibrating metal field start the action.
Exclusive Superbowl field, 2-tier grandstand and scoreboard. Each team includes 11 plastic players with steerable "legs", molded in five 3-D positions plus a triple-threat quarterback. Automatic timer starts and stops with each play. Magnetic 10-yard marker with ball and down indicator and goal-line flags. UL listed, 110–120-v., 60-Hz. AC, 6 watts. 6-ft. cord.
79 N 65131C—Shpg. wt. 8 lbs. $14.94

IMPORTANT NOTE: Games (1 thru 3) not recommended for ages under 8.

Two exciting NFL teams clash on a 26½x15½-inch playing field **$9.97**

2. "Tell" each player where to move with Total Team Control, as in (1) above. Vibrating metal field has 2-tier grandstand and scoreboard. Each team has 11 plastic players molded in five 3-D positions plus a triple-threat quarterback. Automatic timer, magnetic 10-yard marker with ball and down indicator and goal-line flags. UL listed, 110–120-v., 60-Hz. AC, 6 watts.
79 N 65129C—6-ft. cord. Shipping weight 5 pounds $9.97

Two NFL teams collide on a 31½x17½-inch playing field **$12.97**

3. Features the same Total Team Control as Superbowl game above. Vibrating metal field includes a 2-tier grandstand and scoreboard. All 22 plastic players are molded in five 3-D positions plus 2 triple-threat quarterbacks. Includes an automatic timer, magnetic 10-yard marker with ball and down indicator and goal-line flags. UL listed, 110–120-v., 60-Hz. AC, 6 watts, 6-foot cord.
79 N 65212C—Shipping weight 8 pounds $12.97

Great low price for O.J. Simpson See-Action Football Game

WISH BOOK **VALUE**
Only **$8.77** without batteries

4. Each player chooses one of 14 color play slides. Offense and defense slides are projected together .. and you see how the play comes out. Over 288 play possibilities. 19x15x10½ in. high. Uses 4 "D" batteries, order pkg. below.
49 N 65224—Ages 7 and up. Shpg. wt. 3 lbs. 15 oz. $8.77

"D" Batteries. Package of six.
49 N 46995—Shipping weight 1 lb. 4 oz. .... Pkg. $1.49

Pro Draft $6.17

5. Use football trading cards to build a winning team in the draft. Plastic football-shaped card tray, spinner, 1 set of option, player, value, contract cards, 3 or 4 players. Ages 9 and up.
49 N 65031—Wt. 2 lbs. $6.17

NFL Strategy .. a challenge for great football minds like yours
$15.97

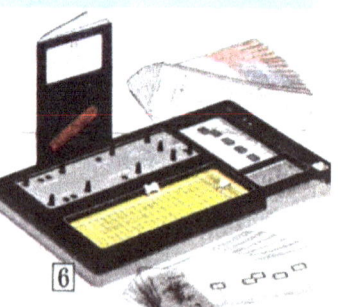

6. Use an authentic NFL playbook .. with 34 offensive and 12 defensive alignments to create realistic game situations. You can pass, run, shift your line and even blitz. Timer mechanism lets you play against the clock .. you can even call time outs. Probability selector gives the statistical results of each play. Plastic frame. 14½x8⅞ inches wide. Ages 12 and up.
49 N 65594—Shpg. wt. 3 lbs. 8 oz. $15.97

NFL Strategy Jr. Like game above, only a smaller, less difficult scale. Incl. NFL playbook with 16 offensive, 16 defensive alignments and probability selector. Plastic. 14½x9 in. wide. Ages 8 and up.
49 N 65218—Shipping weight 2 lbs. $8.99

Monday Night Football by Aurora
$9.77 without battery

7. Select the offense and defense .. over 1480 play possibilities. Push "readout" button .. field lights up showing play results. 21x16x5-in. high plastic field. Uses 1 "AA" battery, order below.
79 N 65711C—Ages 8 and up. Wt. 4 lbs. $9.77

"AA" Batteries. Package of four.
49 N 46991—Shipping weight 4 ounces .... Pkg. 69c

1974 Montgomery Ward

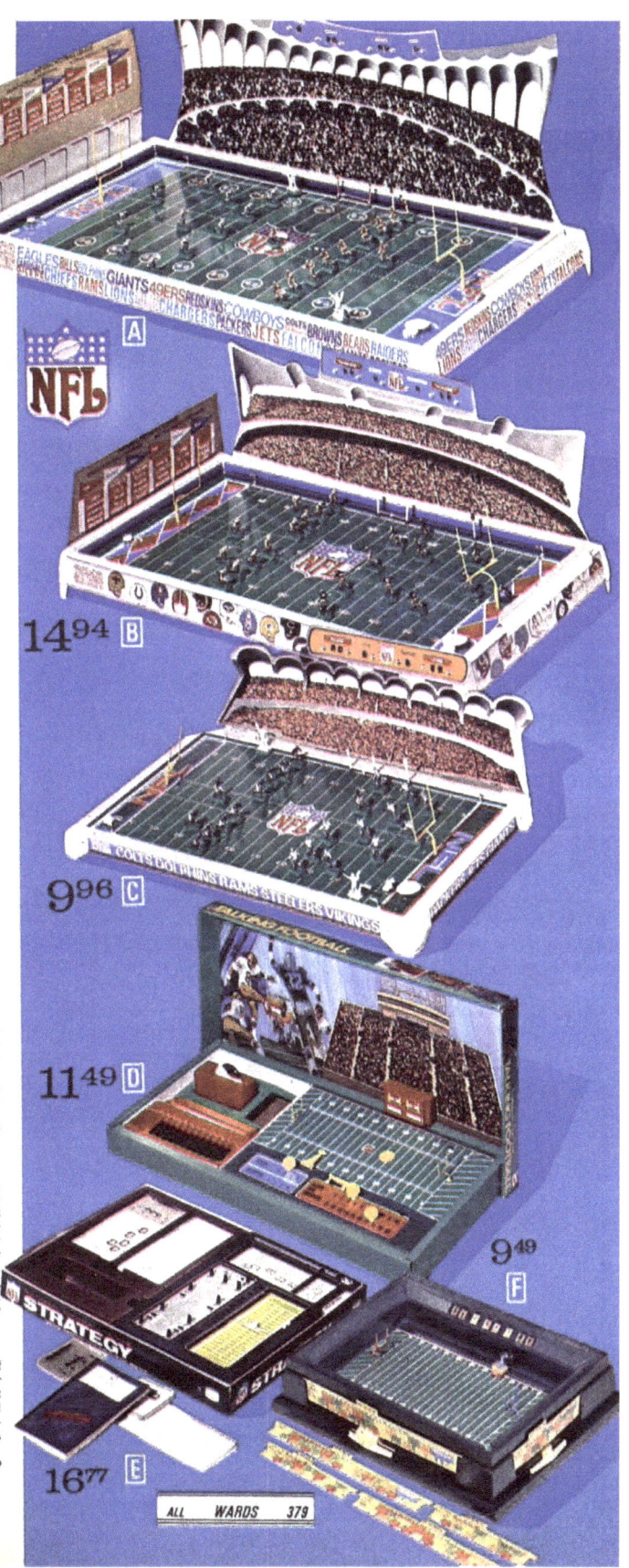

TABLE MODEL ELECTRIC FOOTBALL ...3 CHOICES!

NFL Electric Football Games (A)-(C) have these features:
- 22 pre-painted players in 5 authentic positions, that run real traps, end arounds, sweeps, slants and swing patterns
- Two triple-threat quarterbacks that kick, pass and run
- Automatic timer that starts and stops with each play
- Magnetic first down marker with movable 10-yd. chain
- 4 colorful goal line flags • Authentic NFL goal posts
- UL Listed safety plug and exclusive heavy-duty switch
- Easy to apply identification numbers for each player
- Rugged steel gameboard • Magnetic ball and down marker
- Colorful grandstand with adjustable scoreboard

Deluxe Electric Football
17⁹⁹

A Wards Exclusive NFL Electric Football Game, with your choice of teams. YOU be the coach! Total team control lets you mastermind every run, kick, and block! Wheel in the base of each player lets you pre-program speed and direction of his legs, to obey your commands! You get your home team and opposing team; see below. Jumbo size playing field about 37¾x20¾x3 in. Includes NFL Playbook written by NFL staff, deluxe grandstand, and league standings board. For ages 8 yrs. and up.
48 G 14564 M—Ship. wt. 11 lbs.....................17.99

B Wards Exclusive! Our most popular NFL electric football game. Slightly smaller field than (A): about 31½x17¼x3 in. just the right size for a card table. Includes standings board, scoreboard, Play book and choice of teams (below). For ages 8 yrs. and up.
48 G 14565 M—Ship. wt. 8 lbs. 4 oz.................14.94

When you order (A) or (B) you get these teams:

If you order from	You get these teams
Albany	Jets/Giants
Baltimore	Redskins/Cowboys
Chicago	Bears/Lions
Denver	Rams/49'ers
Ft. Worth	Redskins/Cowboys
Kansas City	Chiefs/Cards
Oakland	Raiders/Chargers
Portland	Rams/49'ers
St. Paul	Vikings/Packers

C Budget NFL electric football game. Playing field about 27x16 in. Teams: Bears and Lions. Does not include Play book, standings board or choice of teams. For ages 8 yrs. and up.
48 G 14539 M—Ship. wt. 4 lbs. 8 oz..................9.96

Talking Football Game

D Sports announcer calls the play-by-play action. It's tough gridiron competition as each player selects his team's strategy. 13 interchangeable records with numerous different plays. Offense chooses one of recorded plays to move ball down the field. Defense counteracts the quarterback's strategy. Then the spectators hear the action. Includes everything you need: record player, records, rack, spin-dial scoreboard, moving football, markers and goal posts. About 31x15 in. overall. Operates on one "D" battery, not included, order on pg. 398. For ages 5 yrs. and up.
48 G 14604 M—Ship. wt. 3 lbs. 14 oz................11.49

NFL Strategy for Football Fans

E Includes official NFL Playbook written by NFL staff which describes all plays, and provides tips on when and how to use them... over 6,000 possible plays! You can run, pass, blitz or shift your line. Adjustable score board; full playing field with movable ball that can be shifted laterally to play hash marks. Revolutionary probability selector determines result of each play instantly! Play against clock, which advances automatically after each down. Play-selector window lets you see actual play diagram of action. Rugged plastic frame 14½x8⅞ in. For ages 12 yrs. and older.
48 G 14566—Ship. wt. 3 lbs. 8 oz...................16.77

Monday Night Football

F Over 1480 different play possibilities, fully computerized! Full of thrills and excitement right up to last remaining seconds! After offensive and defensive plays are chosen, players push read-out button and instantaneous results light up on the playing field surface. Includes players, markers, goal posts and built-in scoreboard. About 21x5x16 in. Requires two "AA" batteries. Order on pg. 398. For ages 8 yrs. and up.
48 G 14536 M—Ship. wt. 4 lbs......................9.49

SAVE THIS CATALOG!
All toys are available until August 31, 1975

1974 J.C. Penney

NFL Electric Football with Total Team Control

You can control the direction of every player (and the triple-threat quarterback can kick, pass, and run!

See Quick Index of NFL items on page 256.

You Call Each Play Because You Set the Direction of Each Player Separately—it's Total Team Control

"Tell" Each Player Where to Move—It's Total Team Control. Just set the wheel in the base of each player for direction, adjust speed control on field, switch on the game, and watch the vibrating metal field start the action. Automatic timer starts and stops each play; scoreboard on grandstand posts game score. Each team has 11 plastic players molded in 5 realistic 3-D football poses; the triple-threat quarterback can kick, pass, and run! Magnetic first down marker, movable 10-yard marker, magnetic ball, goalposts, flags. Operates on 110-120 volts, AC, UL listed. Caution: electric toy—see note on page 413.

Championship Playoffs—Dolphins vs. Raiders; Vikings vs. Cowboys on a 37¾ x 20½-in. Playing Field **17.77**

[A] Dolphins, Raiders, Vikings, Cowboys—four teams, 44 players, plus extra stick-on numbers for favorite player identification. 3-tier grandstand; interchangeable team name cards to keep track of team standings in all divisions. Not mailable to 1st Class P.O.s: see page 307—wt. 11 lbs.
X 923-4220 A 17.77

Vikings battle Chiefs on a 31½ x 17½-in. Playing Field **13.77**

[B] Vikings vs. Chiefs—22 players. 2-tier grandstand; scoreboard posts downs and score. Not mailable to 1st Class P.O.s: see page 307—wt. 8.20 lbs.
X 923-4212 A 13.77

Dolphins and Packers clash on a 26½ x 15½-in. Playing Field **9.77**

[C] Dolphins vs. Packers—22 players. 2-tier grandstand.
X 923-4196 A—Mailable: wt. 4.50 lbs. 9.77

D-Cell Batteries. Package of 6. Mailable: wt. 1.40 lbs.
X 957-1761 A .... Order 1 Pkg. for 1.39

AA-Cell Batteries. Package of 4. Mailable: wt. 0.40 lb.
X 957-1902 A .... Order 1 Pkg. for 89c

Big Action Games On a Play-at-Home Scale

Play Strategy Football ... Over 6,000 Plays!
Patented Probability Selector that gives instant, statistically correct results. NFL playbook with 34 offensive and 12 defensive plays, plus coaching tips. Timer mechanism lets you play against the clock—even call time out! Movable ball. For ages 12 to adult.
X 923-4281 A—Mailable: wt. 3.50 lbs. 15.88

New Pro-Draft Football
Try to Build Your Own Dream Team with official football trading cards. All players of this game are wily franchise holders trying to get together a winning team. Football-shaped plastic card tray with spinner, 4 team trays, cards. 3 to 4 players, ages 9 to adult.
X 923-3446 A—Mailable: wt. 3.50 lbs. 5.99

1975 J.C. Penney

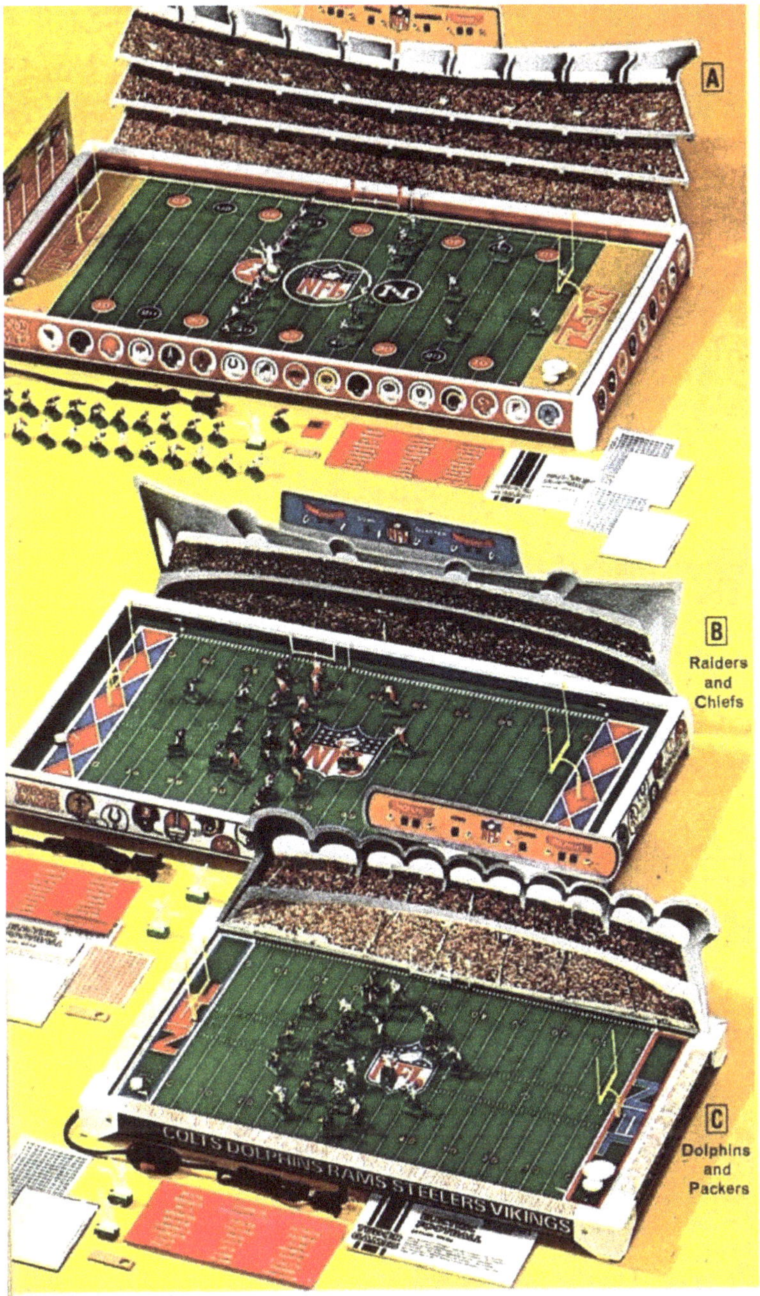
A
B
Raiders and Chiefs
C
Dolphins and Packers
COLTS DOLPHINS RAMS STEELERS VIKINGS

NFL Electric Football with Total Team Control

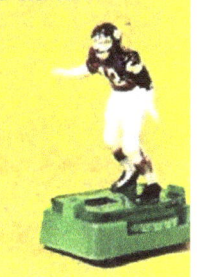

You can control the direction of every player (and the triple-threat quarterback can kick, pass, and run!)

You Call Each Play Because You Set the Direction of Each Player Separately!

"Tell" Each Player Where to Move—It's Total Team Control! Just set the wheel in the base of each player for direction, adjust speed control on field, switch on the game, and watch the vibrating metal field start the action. Automatic timer starts and stops with each play; scoreboard on paperboard grandstand to show game score, downs and quarter. Each team has 11 plastic players molded in 5 realistic 3-D football poses, painted in official NFL team colors; the triple-threat quarterback can kick, pass, and run! Magnetic first down marker with movable 10-yard marker, magnetic ball, goalposts, 4 goal-line flags. Easy-to-apply player numbers (2 through 89) operate on 110–120 volts, AC, UL listed. Caution: electric toy—see note on page 425.

Championship Playoffs with 4 teams 37x20-in. Playing Field 19.88

[A] **Steelers, Raiders, Vikings, Rams**—four teams, 44 players, including two quarterbacks, all with bases. Interchangeable team name-cards to keep track of team standings in all divisions. Not mailable to 1st Class P.O.'s: see page 327—wt. 11 lbs.
X 923-4220 A 19.88

Raiders battle Chiefs on a 31x17-in. Playing Field 15.88

[B] **Raiders vs. Chiefs—22 players.** Post downs, quarter and score on grandstand scoreboard. Not mailable to 1st Class P.O.'s: see page 327—wt. 8.20 lbs.
X 923-4212 A 15.88

Dolphins and Packers clash on a 26x15-in. Playing Field 11.88

[C] **Dolphins vs. Packers**—22 players.
X 923-4196 A—Mailable: wt. 4.50 lbs. 11.88

SAVE THIS CATALOG—order anything on this page until August 14, 1976

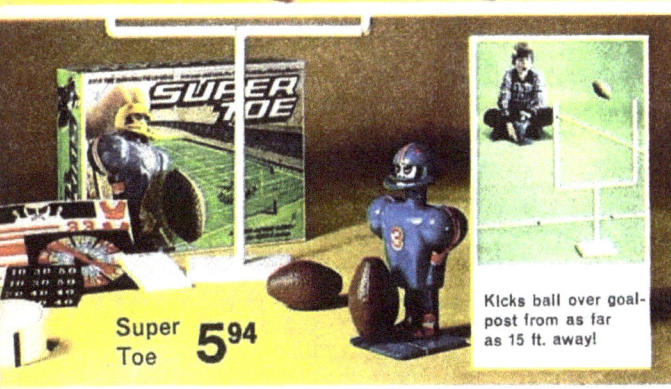

SUPER TOE
Super Toe 5.94
Kicks ball over goal-post from as far as 15 ft. away!

Pro-Draft Football
6.87
PRO DRAFT

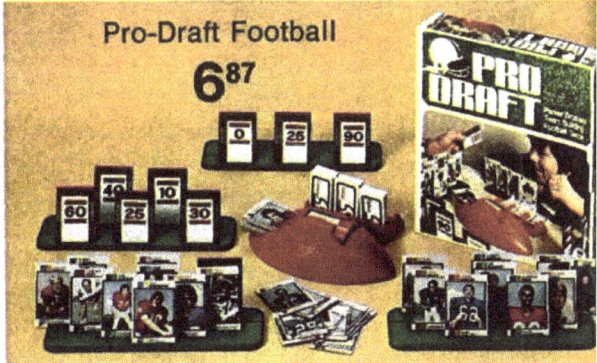

1975 Sears

$15.97

Super Bowl Electric Football Game
NFL's Steelers and Vikings clash on
31½x17½-inch playing gridiron

Sold only at Sears. Total Team Control lets you "tell" each player what pattern to run, what defender to block, to make the play "go all the way". Switch on the game and watch the vibrating metal field start the action.

Exclusive Super Bowl field, 2-tier grandstand and scoreboard. Each team includes 11 plastic players with official uniforms and steerable "legs", molded in five 3-D positions plus a triple-threat quarterback. Automatic timer starts and stops. Magnetic 10-yard marker with ball and down indicator and goal line flags. UL listed; 110-120-volt, 60 Hz. AC. 6 watts. 6-foot cord. Ages 8 and up.
79 C 65538C—Shipping weight 8 pounds $15.97

$8.87

Electric Football Game

Two teams clash on a 26½x15½-inch playing field. "Tell" each player where to move with Total Team Control. Vibrating metal field has grandstand and scoreboard. Each team has 11 plastic players molded in five 3-D positions plus a triple-threat quarterback. Automatic timer, 10-yard marker, down indicator, flags. UL listed; 110-120-v., 60-Hz. AC. 6 watts. 6-foot cord. Ages 8 years and up.
79 C 65536C—Shipping weight 4 pounds $8.87

$16.68

NFL Strategy

Use an authentic NFL playbook . . with 34 offensive and 12 defensive alignments. You can pass, run, shift your line and even blitz. Timer mechanism lets you play against the clock. Probability selector gives the statistical results of each play. Plastic frame. 14½x8⅞ inches wide. Ages 14 years and up.
49 C 65594—Wt. 3 lbs. 8 oz $16.68

$8.97

Electric Baseball

"Pitcher" throws balls, strikes and even change-ups. Batter can swing away, bunt or walk. Outfield "arm" tries to throw baserunners out. Metal 20x20-inch ballpark in official colors. Adjustable scoreboard. UL listed; 110-120-v., 60-Hz. AC. 6 watts. 6-ft. cord. Ages 8 and up.
79 C 65072C—Wt. 5 lbs. $8.97

542 [Sears] co   NOTE: Electrical items not recommended for children under 8

Our Best Professional Hockey Game

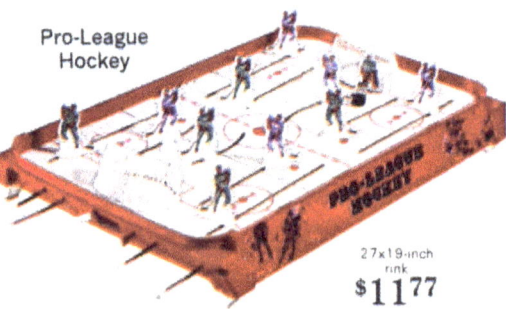

36x21-inch rink
$14.99

36x21-inch rink is the center for gear-driven polypropylene players to skate, check, pass, shoot and score . . just by pulling, pushing and twirling rods at your end of the rink. Delayed-action overhead puck-dropper and score indicators. Fast-action roller-bearing puck. Hardboard, plastic and metal. Extra team sets below. Ages 6 and up.
79 C 65533L—Wt. 9 lbs. If mailed takes 10-lb. rate, see p. 276 . . . $14.99

Extra Players. Ten (60 players) teams per set. Polypropylene.
49 C 65801—West Division (including Canada). Wt. 12 oz. . . Set $3.99
49 C 65802—East Division (including Russia). Wt. 12 oz. . . . Set 3.99

Pro-League Hockey

27x19-inch rink
$11.77

Two pro-league teams provide the action on this 27x19-inch rink. Using your skill, push, pull and twirl the rods at your end to make plastic players pass the puck, shoot and score. Game includes puck return chute and a fast-action wooden puck. Constructed of metal, hardboard and plastic. For hockey buffs ages 6 years and up.
79 C 65134C—Shipping weight 7 pounds $11.77

$4.77   **$5.89**

Bop Hockey

1 This game uses the cushion sides and corners of the slick "rink" to send the puck where you want it. Guarding "goalie" never budges as your shots whiz across the 23¼x15⅝-inch rink, sending puck spinning if inaccurate. Plastic. 2 sticks and roller-bearing puck. Rules. Ages 3 and up.
Shipping weight 3 lbs.
79 C 65601C $4.77

Face-Off Hockey Management Game

2 Face-Off. A slapstick game about hockey management. You play the owner of the team. In the scramble for superstars to build up the strongest team, you have to be shrewd and manage your cash as well. Play a full season of hockey along the way to see how your efforts pay off. 2 to 4 players. Ages 9 and up.
49 C 65608—Wt. 2 lbs $5.89

1975 Montgomery Ward

Electronic Pinball 22.94

Command Control™ Electric Football 14.88

Fabulous Value

Become the pinball wizard of your neighborhood! Battery operated pinball makes a perfect addition to your gameroom. Pull the lever and ball travels through obstacle course. Spinner activates ... bells ring ... score as high as 100,000! Sophisticated features of a professional game: submarine loading; 2 replay flippers. 29x14x43 in. H. Uses 4 "D" batteries, not incl., order pg. 369. For children 6 yrs. and older.
48 T 14667 M—Ship. wt. 19 lbs. 22.94

Extra point conversions! End sweeps! Quarterback sneaks! This game does it all. Direct-O-Matic™ lets you set the direction of each player separately. Develop your own game plan with the exclusive Strategy Play Formations. Also features: control action levers for each team; 2 action quarterbacks that really kick and pass; 3-dimension grandstand; magnetic footballs; vibrating field with variable speed control; scoreboard, goal posts, yard markers and flags; sturdy floor stand. UL listed. 38x21 in.
48 T 14577 M—Ship. wt. 16 lbs. 14.88

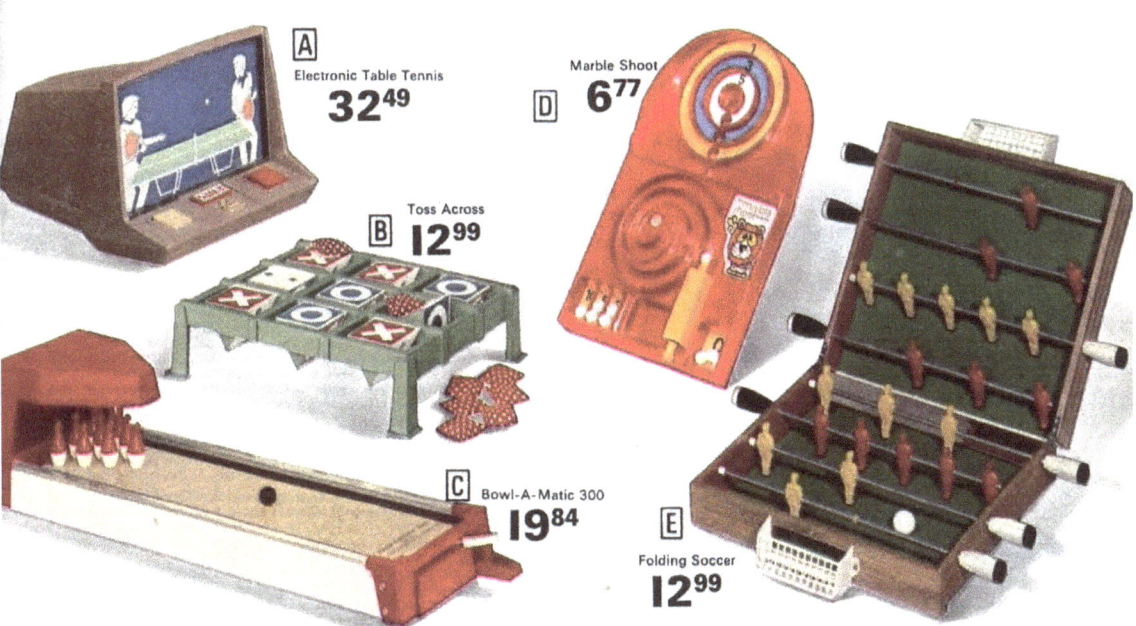

[A] **Electronic Table Tennis** 32.49

[B] **Toss Across** 12.99

[C] **Bowl-A-Matic 300** 19.84

[D] **Marble Shoot** 6.77

[E] **Folding Soccer** 12.99

A You'll need quick reflexes to beat your opponent in this game. "Ball" bounces back and forth on the screen. Ball must be hit the second it reaches your paddle ... just push the button. Server also controls the speed of the ball. Uses 4 "D" batteries, not incl.—order pg. 369. 17x13x13 in.
48 T 14086 M—For children 7 yrs. and up. Ship. wt. 10 lbs. 32.49

B Beanbag version of Tic-Tac-Toe. Play indoors or out. Hit rotating symbols with beanbag to turn up "X" or "O." First player or team to line up 3 in a row, wins. Includes plastic frame on legs and 8 polka-dotted bean bags. About 22x18½ in. For children 6 yrs. older, and adults.
48 T 14520 M—Ship. wt. 6 lbs. 10 oz. 12.99

C The great game you've seen on TV. Go for a strike on a real-lite table-top bowling alley —right in your own living room! Remote control Bowl-A-Matic does it all—the amazing automatic pin-setter sets 'em up; automatic ball return lets you play hour after hour. Colorful molded pins are individually activated by fast moving ball. Solid wood-style construction, precision smooth alley. About 45x13 in. For fans 5 yrs. and up.
48 T 14883 M—Partially assembled. Ship. wt. 19 lbs. 19.84

D Have hours of fun competing with your friends, or "play" against yourself trying to beat your last score! Spring loaded plunger shoots marbles through the swirl-shaped launch chute, over and into the scoring holes. Marble then automatically returns so you can keep a record of your score ... 0, 1, 3, 5, or 10. Comes with 10 marbles and detachable legs. For children 3 yrs. and up. 15½x9¾x2¼ in.
48 T 14670—Made in Japan. Ship. wt. 2 lbs. 11 oz. 6.77

E Official size team action! You control your team with telescoping rods to kick, fake and move from side to side while your opponent is doing the same. While you are trying to watch 22 men, the excitement continues to rise as you both plan your strategy to battle it out and score. Use on tabletop. Folds in half so you can carry it with you anywhere. Sturdy hardwood construction. About 30x16 in. Includes 2 balls. Not recommended for children under 3 yrs.
48 T 14682—Ship. wt. 7 lbs. 12.99

1976 Sears

$15.97

Super Bowl 1976 Electric Football Game
Dallas Cowboys vs. Pittsburgh Steelers

Two NFL Teams in official Super Bowl uniforms run plays using your strategies.
HOW TO PLAY: Total Team Control dials in each platform base let you set direction for each player. Tackles, ends, guards, backs, in five poses, move left, right or straight, make sharp turns, wide arcs or end sweeps. Switch on game and field vibrates sending players off in your patterns. You set the pace for each play with speed-control dial. Automatic timer starts and stops with each play. Players may be removed from bases for strategy sessions or display.

WHAT YOU GET: Metal gridiron playing field 31⅝x17⅜x3 in. high. Grandstand 12 in. high with adjustable scoreboard. 24 plastic figures with 2 triple-threat quarterbacks, magnetic 10-yd. marker with movable chain marker, magnetic ball, down marker, 4 goal line flags.
ELECTRICAL INFORMATION: UL listed; 110–120-volt, 60-Hz. AC. 6 watts. 6-foot cord. Not recommended for ages under 8.
FOR AGES: 8 years and up.
ORDERING INFORMATION:
79 N 65538C—Shpg. wt. 8 lbs.........$15.97

Electric Football Game

HOW TO PLAY: Total Team Control bases determine movement in each figure. Players move left, right, straight, making sharp turns, wide arcs or sweeps. 2 quarterbacks carry ball, pass and kick by hand lever. Switch on and metal field vibrates sending players off. You control speed with dial, automatic timer starts, stops with each play.
WHAT YOU GET: Metal field, 26⁷⁄₁₆x15⅜ in. wide, stand with scoreboard, 24 plastic players, 10-yd. marker, down indicator.
ELECTRICAL INFO: UL listed; 110–120-v., 60-Hz. AC. 6 w. 6-ft. cord. Not for ages under 8.
FOR AGES: 8 years and up.
ORDERING INFORMATION:
79 N 65536C—Shpg. wt. 4 lbs. $9.97

$9.97

"Batter up" with two baseball-pinball games

Big Bat Baseball™ $11.94

Hit 'n Run Pinball $12.33

NFL Strategy $11.97

Electro Bowl $14.99 without batteries

$10.87

Electric Baseball

HOW TO PLAY: Pitch, field via 2 spring-action levers; opponent hits with spring-action bat, switches on vibrating field to send players around bases.
WHAT YOU GET: 20x20-in. metal field, 4 base runners, scoreboard, grandstand.
ELECTRICAL INFO: UL listed; 110–120-volt, 60-Hz. AC. 6 watts. 6-foot cord. Not recommended for ages under 8 years.
FOR AGES: 8 years and up.
ORDERING INFORMATION:
79 N 65072C—Shpg. wt. 5 lbs. ..$10.87

$5.33

Bas-Ket . . . levers flip the ball into the net

Here's play action for any "cage" fan.
HOW TO PLAY: Control shots from any position on the court with mechanical levers. Up to 6 players can sink shots.
WHAT YOU GET: Fiberboard (not wood or hardboard) court 20x12 in. wide, 2 scoreboard-backboards, plastic ball. Rules.
FOR AGES: 4 years and up.
ORDERING INFORMATION:
49 N 6502—Wt. 2 lbs. 12 oz. $5.33

1976 Montgomery Ward

Electric Football **14⁸⁸**

Drive Game **14⁴⁹**

Electric Tennis **23⁸⁸**

Push-button Soccer **8⁹⁹**

Tin Can Alley™ **27⁸⁸**

Folding Soccer **14⁹⁹**

Pele Air Soccer **36⁸⁸**

Exploding Bridge Game **4⁹⁹**

WINNERS!

9 You're in the driver's seat as you steer car on revolving roadway avoiding hazards and making split-second decisions. High impact plastic; 13x17x6½ in.; 4-position gear shift. From Japan.
48 G 14889—Order 3 "D" batteries, page 409. Wt. 5 lbs. 6 oz. 14.49

10 Extra point conversions! End sweeps! Quarterback sneaks! Direct-O-Matic™ lets you set the direction of each player separately. Also features: control action levers; 2 action quarterbacks; grandstand; magnetic footballs; vibrating field with variable speed control; scoreboard; accessories. Table model; 38x21 in. UL listed.
48 G 14578 A—Ship. wt. 11 lbs. 8 oz. ..... A Fabulous Value at 14.88

11 Fast, fun game—serve, volley and score! Keep your eye on the ball as you control "rackets" with knobs. Automatic scoreboard and bell visually and audibly record score up to 10 points. High impact plastic; 19½x11 in. Order 4 "D" batteries, page 409.
48 G 14599—From Japan. Ship. wt. 5 lbs. 23.88

12 Pass, kick and score against your opponent—but don't forget to guard your goal! Fast action play with push-button controls. 19½x9⅞x3¼ in. metal game board; 22 plastic players; 3 balls.
48 G 14693—From Hong Kong. Ship. wt. 3 lbs. 12 oz. 8.99

13 Plan your strategy, battle it out and score! You and your opponent control your teams with telescoping rods to kick, fade and move from side to side. Table top model folds in half—carry it anywhere. Sturdy hardwood construction; 30x16 in.; 2 balls. Not recommended for children under 3 years.
48 G 14682—Ship. wt. 7 lbs. ..... A Fabulous Value at 14.99

14 Realistic target rifle "shoots" beam of light—when you hit the knothole in fence, can falls over. Safety engineered; no bullets or darts. Some assembly needed. Order 4 "C", 3 "D" batt., page 409.
48 G 14030 M—Age 8 and up. Ship. wt. 6 lbs. 6 oz. 27.88

15 Enjoy all the thrills and competition of Pele professional soccer! Forceful streams of air from blower whirl your uniformed teams—spinning, kicking and passing the ball. Directable air power; exclusive power play bumpers; swivel action goalie. Table model; 40x 21¼ in. Durable wood construction; 4 balls.
48 G 14077 M—UL listed. Ship. wt.'25 lbs. 36.88

16 Get your marble through the obstacle filled battleground and across the bridge before "time bomb" goes off and bridge explodes. Last one across wins! High impact plastic; 16x7½ in.
48 G 14892—From Japan. Ship. wt. 1 lb. 12 oz. 4.99

1976 J.C. Penney

NFL Electric Football with Total Team Control
You can control the direction of every player

B Rams and Cowboys

C Dolphins and Jets

D Redskins and Chiefs

[A] NFL Teams. All 28 teams are available—and they fit all these electric football games! Each team has 11 NFL players in five offensive and defensive positions. With Total Team Control bases and identification numbers. *Order by conference and division.* NATIONAL CONFERENCE: East Division (Cardinals, Cowboys, Eagles, Giants, Redskins); West Division (Falcons, 49'ers, Rams, Saints, Seattle Seahawks); and Central Division (Bears, Lions, Packers, Vikings). AMERICAN CONFERENCE: East Division (Bills, Colts, Dolphins, Jets, Patriots); West Division (Broncos, Chargers, Chiefs, Raiders, Tampa Bay Buccaneers); and Central Division (Bengals, Browns, Oilers, Steelers).

National Conference Teams.
X 924-9855 A—Eastern Division........9.98
X 924-9871 A—Western Division.......9.98
X 924-9863 A—Central Division........7.98

American Conference Teams.
X 924-9889 A—Eastern Division........9.98
X 924-9913 A—Western Division.......9.98
X 924-9897 A—Central Division........7.98

"Tell" Each Player Where to Move—it's Total Team Control! Just set the wheel in the base of each player for direction, adjust speed control field, switch on the game, and watch the vibrating metal field start the action. Automatic timer starts and stops with each play; scoreboard on paperboard grandstand to show game score, downs and quarter. Each team has 11 plastic players molded in 5 realistic pro football poses, painted in official NFL team colors; and the triple threat quarterback can kick, pass, and run! Magnetic first down marker with movable 10-yard marker, magnetic ball, goal posts, 4 goal-line flags. Easy-to-apply player numbers (2 through 9). Operates on 110-120 volts, AC, UL listed. Caution: electric toy —see note on page 463. For ages 8 and up.

Championship Playoffs with 2 teams, 37x20-in. Playing Field   19.88
[B] NFL Conference Championship with the Rams and the Cowboys. Interchangeable team name-cards to keep track of team standings in all divisions. Not mailable to 1st Class P.O.'s: see page 332—wt. 11 lbs.
X 923-4220 A 19.88

Dolphins battle Jets on a 31x17-in. Playing Field   16.88
[C] Dolphins vs. Jets—22 players. Not mailable to 1st Class P.O.'s: see page 332—wt. 8.20 lbs.
X 923-4212 A 16.88

Redskins and Chiefs clash on a 26x15-in. Playing Field   12.88
[D] Redskins vs. Chiefs—22 players.
X 923-4196 A—Mailable: wt. 4.50 lbs. 12.88

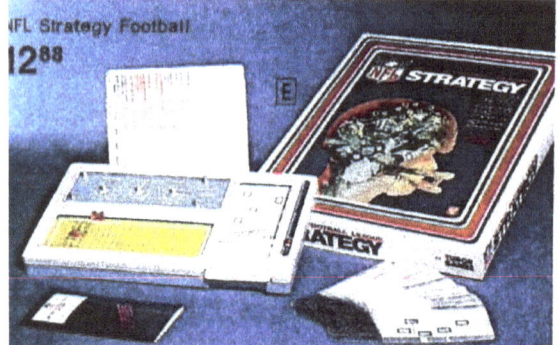

NFL Strategy Football   12.88

[E] NFL Strategy Football, sanctioned by the National Football League. The outcome of plays is controlled by the skill of the players. Patented Probability Selector determines statistically correct results instantaneously. Set includes plastic game case with adjustable scoreboard, play selector and moving field with football marker, NFL Playbook, probability selector, 34 offensive and 12 defensive play diagrams.
924-9848 A—Mailable: wt. 3 lbs. 12.88

[F] Foto-Electric Football   6.99
Foto-Electric Football Game. Choose your offensive; Your opponent sets his defense. Play viewer actually shows "ball carrier" in action until he's stopped. Play results based on actual NFL records. With field and scoreboard, 12 offensive and 6 defensive plays, kicking and run-back dials in full color, 12 offensive, 6 defensive cards, and instructions. 19x15x4¾-in. high. 110-120 volts, AC, UL listed. For ages 10 years to adult. 40 watt bulb included.
X 925-0481 A—Mailable: wt. 4.50 lbs. 6.99

1977 J.C. Penney

NFL Teams. All 28 teams available in official team colors, with number decals. Each team has 11 players—teams have both black and white players molded in 5 different positions. Use with [B] and [C] below, or any Tudor electric football game. Each player comes on a base stand that slides into control base included with games. Order by Conference and Division. NATIONAL CONFERENCE: *East Division* (Cardinals, Cowboys, Eagles, Giants, Redskins); *West Division* (Falcons, 49'ers, Rams, Saints); *Central Division* (Bears, Lions, Packers, Vikings, Tampa Bay Buccaneers). AMERICAN CONFERENCE: *East Division* (Bills, Colts, Dolphins, Jets, Patriots); *West Division* (Broncos, Chargers, Chiefs, Raiders, Seattle Seahawks); *Central Division* (Bengals, Browns, Oilers, Steelers). Mailable: wt. 0.80 lb. each.

National Conference Teams		American Conference Teams	
X 924-9855 A—Eastern	9.98	X 924-9889 A—Eastern	9.98
X 925-9052 A—Western	7.98	X 925-9060 A—Western	9.98
X 925-9045 A—Central	9.98	X 924-9897 A—Central	7.98

[A] Mr. Quarterback— He can throw a pass as far as 30 ft. **17.97**

Play receiver by yourself or with your friends!

Football Fun for the Whole Family

[A] **Mr. Quarterback Football Passer** throws a perfect spiral pass every time! He can throw as far as 30 ft. Play by yourself, one on one, or with a whole team. The mechanical passer has an angle selector for straight or high arc passes, a distance selector for short or long passes, and a built-in timer to delay the pass until you're in position. Soft plastic football—so you can even play indoors. Time delay mechanism has ratchet-lock release. Molded plastic and steel. 11x8½x18½ in. high.
X 925-3659 A—Mailable: wt. 5 lbs. 17.97

[B] & [C] **"Tell" Each Player Where to Move—It's Tudor's Total Team Control!** Just set the wheel in the base of each player for direction, adjust speed control on the field, switch on the game, and watch the vibrating metal field start the action. Automatic timer starts and stops with each play; scoreboard on paperboard grandstand shows score, downs, and quarter. Each team has 11 plastic players in official NFL colors molded in five 3-D action poses. The triple-threat quarterback can kick, pass, and run! Magnetic down marker with movable 10 yard marker, magnetic ball, goal posts, 4 goal-line flags. Easy-to-apply player numbers (2 through 89). Order additional NFL teams at top of this page. UL listed, 110-120V, AC. Caution: electric toy—see note on page 491. For ages 8 and up.

NFL Superbowl
[B] 22 players in official uniforms battle on a 37½x20½-in. playing field.
X 925-3642 A—Mailable: wt. 9.50 lbs. 18.88

NFL Football
[C] 22 players in official uniforms clash on a 26½x15½-in. playing field.
X 923-4196 A—Mailable: wt. 4.50 lbs. 13.88

[D] **NFL Strategy Football**, sanctioned by the National Football League. The success of plays is determined by the skill of the players. The Probability Selector determines statistically correct results instantaneously. Set includes plastic game case with adjustable scoreboard, play selector, and playing field with football marker, NFL Playbook, probability selector, 34 offensive, and 12 defensive play diagrams.
X 924-9848 A—Mailable: wt. 3 lbs. 12.66

[E] **Magnetic NFL Action Darts** stick with magnets, not with points. Handsome steel dart board is really two games in one. One side lets you play football, NFL style. Gain ground, fumble, kick, even be intercepted—the board provides for real football game possibilities. The back is a regulation-size red, white, and blue 20-point-game dart board. Metal board is 19¼x19¼x1½ in. deep. Comes with six 4-in. long magnetic-tipped darts.
X 925-3634 A—Mailable: wt. 3.75 lbs. 6.74

SAVE THIS CATALOG. Order anything on these two pages—at these low prices— until August 12, 1978

NFL Electric Football with Total Team Control You can control the direction of every play and player!

[B] Superbowl Football **18.88**

[C] NFL Football **13.88**

[D] NFL Strategy Football **12.66**

[E] Magnetic NFL Action Darts **6.74**

Traditional dart board on back

1977 Sears

Action Games

[1] NFL Superbowl Electric Football Game $18.49

[2] Electric Football Game $10.22

[3] Electric Baseball $11.47 — Players even run bases

[4] Tudor Rod Hockey $18.49

[5] NFL Action Darts $7.47 — ...with traditional dart game on reverse side

[6] Bas-Ket $5.22

[7] Tudor Bowl $9.47

[8] Battle Ball $10.45

1977 Montgomery Ward

get set for fun!

10 You're in the driver's seat as you steer car on revolving roadway avoiding hazards and making split-second decisions. High impact plastic; 13x17x6½ in.; 4-position gear shift. Japan.
48 T 14889—Order 3 "D" batt., page 335. Ship. wt. 5 lbs. 6 oz.....14.99

11 Battery-operated tank prowls through minefield intent on knocking your tanks out of position. Your only defense—press the button to put up obstacles that turn tank around—toward your enemy. Durable plastic 18x14 in. Hong Kong. Ship. wt. 3 lbs. 8 oz.
48 T 14692—Order 2 "AA" batteries, page 335..................8.99

12 Realistic target rifle "shoots" beam of light—when you hit the knothole in fence, can falls over. Safety engineered; no bullets or darts. Some assembly needed. Order 4 "C", 3 "D" batteries, page 335.
48 T 14030 M—Shipping weight 7 lbs.........................32.88

13 Air-powered 3-dimensional skill and action game requires a steady hand and watchful eye. Maneuver the ball through the stunts with specially designed air-gun. Includes game board, plastic stunts, ball and air-gun. Order 2 "D" batteries on page 335.
48 T 14291—Shipping weight 3 lbs. 8 oz......................11.44

14 Play Tic-Tac-Toe and Ring Toss underwater! Control the motion of rings and balls with Whooshbutton that forces air currents into the tank. Just add tap water to unfilled tank. Ship. wt. 15 oz.
L48 T 14917—State 01, Tic-Tac-Toe or 02, Ring Toss..........each 3.99

15 "Kick" the ball right into your opponent's goal—but watch out! He's using his flippers to defend the goal and try to shoot the ball into yours. Flippers work independently or together. Plastic playing field, 11x18 in. 2 goals, 2 balls included.
48 T 14867—Hong Kong. Ship. wt. 1 lb. 11 oz...................3.99

16 Score your share of strikes and spares on realistic vinyl mat "alley", 20 x 44 in. long. Set pins by pulling tab on top of 21x15-in. plastic control board; as you roll ball to hit rods under board, "pins" drop down. Ball included.
48 T 14902—Hong Kong. Ship. wt. 2 lbs. 6 oz...................5.99

17 Play catch with Harry Hippo, or Snatch with Larry Lobster—just press the Whooshbutton for hours of bubbly fun. Add tap water to 6¼-in. high container and you're ready to play!
48 T 14918—Shipping weight 10 oz....................both for 4.66

18 Extra point conversions! End sweeps! Quarterback sneaks! Direct-O-Matic™ lets you set the direction of each player separately. Also features: control action levers; 2 action quarterbacks; grandstand; magnetic footballs; vibrating field with variable speed control; scoreboard; accessories. Table model; 38x21 in. UL listed. Wt. 11 lbs. 8 oz.
48 T 14578 A—A great gift buy from Wards for only.............14.99

59

1978 Sears

Punt, kick and tackle to score a touchdown in ELECTRIC FOOTBALL

NFL Superbowl Electric Football Game $19.99

$8.47

$11.47

NFL Quarterback $8.47

NFL Strategy Football $16.44

(1) Rod Hockey. Gear-driven players skate, check, pass, shoot and score . . . operate them by pulling, pushing, twisting rods at your end of rink. Delayed-action puck drop keeps game fair.
CONSTRUCTION: Hardboard, plastic and metal rink. 37 3/4 x 21 1/8 x 3 5/8 in. high.
ACCESS: 12 safety plastic figures. Combination period-board, puck drop. Includes 1 puck.
FOR AGES: 8 years and up.
ORDER INFO: Partly assembled. Instr. If mailed, takes 15-lb. rate, see p. 330.
79 N 62036L—Shpg. wt. 11 lbs. . . . $18.97

(2 and 3) Electric Football Games. Total Team Control dial in base of each player determines movement. Players in 5 poses. Switch on game and field vibrates. Speed control dial. Automatic timer starts and stops with each play.
ELECTRICAL INFO: UL listed; 110-120-v., 60-Hz. AC. 6 watts. 5-ft. cord. Not recommended for ages under 8 years.
FOR AGES: 8 years and up.

(2) NFL Superbowl Electric Football Game. Officially licensed product.
CONSTRUCTION: Metal playing field 31 5/8 x 17 5/8 x 3 inches high. 3 1/2-inch high adjustable scoreboard.
ACCESSORIES: 22 plastic figures plus 2 triple-threat quarterbacks, magnetic 10-yd. marker with movable chain marker, rubber balls, down marker.
ORD INFO: Partly assembled. Instr.
79 N 62034C—Shpg. wt. 8 lbs. . . . $19.99

(3) Electric Football Game.
CONSTR: Metal field 26 7/16 x 15 3/8 x 1 7/8 in. high.
ACCESS: Scoreboard with stand, 24 plastic players, 10-yd. marker, down indicator.
ORDER INFO: Partly assembled. Instr.
79 N 65536C—Shpg. wt. 4 lbs. . . . $11.47

(4) Extra NFL Teams for electric football games. Officially licensed product. 11 figures per team. 4 or 5 teams in division in their team colors. Figures attach to Total Control base (not included).
ORDERING INFORMATION:
49 N 62699—4 AFC Central Div. Teams
49 N 62701—4 NFC West Div. Teams
Shpg. wt. 6 oz. . . . $7.97
49 N 62702—5 AFC East Div. Teams
49 N 62703—5 AFC West Div. Teams
49 N 62705—5 NFC Central Div. Teams
49 N 62704—5 NFC East Div. Teams
Shpg. wt. 6 oz. . . . $9.97

(5) NFL Quarterback. Officially licensed product. Choose from 20 offensive and 8 defensive plays . . . each with 5 different results all statistically correct. All plays are accurately diagrammed and color coded.
CONSTRUCTION: Paper chipboard playing surface is 16x12 1/2 in. wide.
ACCESS: Scoreboard, sliding 10-yd. ball marker, NFL playbook.
FOR AGES: 8 years to adult.
ORDERING INFORMATION:
49 N 62698—Shpg. wt. 1 lb. 12 oz. . $8.47

(6) NFL Strategy Football. Officially licensed product. Select from 42 offensive and 12 defensive alignments . . . 7,560 different ways a play can turn out. Probability selector gives statistical results.
CONSTR: Plastic surface, 14 1/2 x 9 in.
ACCESS: Scoreboard, NFL playbook, timer.
FOR AGES: 8 years to adult.
ORDERING INFORMATION:
49 N 6526—Shpg. wt. 3 lbs. . . . $16.44

(7) Tudor Bowl. Throw ball down "alley"; returns automatically. Dual action pin reset.
CONSTRUCTION: One-piece metal housing unit. Realistic wood-grain enameled alley, 15 1/4 x 11 5/8 x 9 1/8 in. high.
ACCESS: Ten 4 1/2-in. high plastic pins, 3-in. diam. polyethylene ball.
FOR AGES: 8 years and up.
ORDER INFO: Partly assembled. Instr.
79 N 62037C—Shpg. wt. 4 lbs. . . . $10.44

(8) Bas-Ket. Control shots from any position with mechanical levers. Up to 6 players.
CONSTR: 20x12 in. wide fiberboard (not wood or hardboard) court.
ACCESSORIES: 2 scoreboard backboards, plastic ball, rules.
FOR AGES: 4 years and up.
ORDERING INFORMATION:
49 N 6502—Shpg. wt. 2 lbs. 4 oz. . . . $5.94

(9) Electric Baseball. Pitch, field using 2 spring-action levers; opponent hits with spring-action bat, switch on vibrating field to send players around bases.
CONSTR: 19 5/16 x 19 5/16-in. metal field.
ACCESS: 4 base runners, 7 7/8-in. high grandstand with scoreboard.
ELECTRICAL INFO: UL listed; 110-120-volt. 60 Hz AC. 6 watts. 5-foot cord. Not recommended for ages under 8.
FOR AGES: 8 years and up.
ORDER INFO: Partly assembled. Instr.
79 N 65072C—Shpg. wt. 5 lbs. . . . $12.47

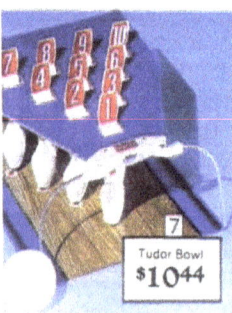

Tudor Bowl $10.44

Bas-Ket levers flip the ball into the net $5.94

Electric Baseball $12.47

Players even run bases

GAMES

1978 Montgomery Ward

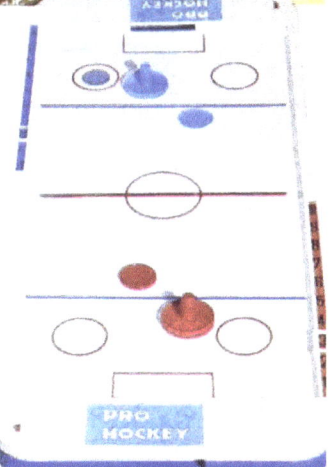

WHAT'S YOUR GAME?
Wards nine-page Game Shop starts here!

A Talking ABC® Monday Night Football. "Call the play, hear it happen!" Offensive player chooses one of 10 offensive play records; defensive player selects one of 6 defenses. Insert record into voice unit; hear sportscaster call the play-by-play. 60 play possibilities like "end around", "blitz", "quarterback sneak", etc. Includes voice unit, 13 records, 18½x9¼-in. gameboard, scoreboard, label sheet, instructions. Order one "D" battery, page 377.
48 G 14604—Ship. wt. 2 lbs. 1 oz. **9⁹⁵**

B NFL Super Bowl Electric Football. You're the coach for exciting action as you mastermind every run, kick and block! 22 authentically uniformed players (Cowboys and Broncos) in 5 realistic poses. Total Team Control lets you set the direction of every player. Rugged steel gameboard (16x32 in.), adjustable scoreboard, magnetic ball and down marker, magnetic first down marker with 10-yard chain. Automatic timer starts and stops with each play; speed control with printed dial. Player I.D. numbers incl. UL listed safety plug and exclusive heavy-duty switch.
48 G 14552—Ship. wt. 8 lbs. **18⁸⁴**

C Folding Soccer. The action is fast and furious in stimulating soccer game. Built to last through a family of kids, sturdy hardwood case for storage. Plan your strategy, battle it out and score! You and your opponent control teams with telescoping rods to kick, fade and move from side to side. 30x16 inches; 2 balls.
48 G 14682—From Brazil. Ship. wt. 7 lbs. . . . **15⁹⁹**

D Power-Jet™ Hockey. Puck is friction-less—floats on a cushion of air. It takes fast reflexes to keep up with your opponent in this game! Play against time—timer automatically records two minutes time per period for three periods of exciting action. Built-in scorekeepers and fast action rebound puck. Perforated bed with high-impact styrene surface. Molded plastic corners. Steel folding legs. About 54x22x30 in. high. UL listed; CSA approved blower.
48 G 14623 M—Mailable. Ship. wt. 36 lbs. . . **47⁸⁸**

E The Champ from Coleco. 45-inch pool table is built to last with strong steel legs. Live-action cushions and smooth cloth covered surface. Single-end ball return. Side rack for scoring, storing accessories. 2 cues; 1-inch balls; triangle. 45x22x26 inches high. NOTE: When measuring space for pool table, allow at least 3 feet of playing area around table.
48 G 14664 M—Mailable. Ship. wt. 24 lbs. . . **26⁸⁸**

F Battery-powered air-activated Pro Hockey Game. Enjoy the speed, thrills and excitement of professional hockey as you send your puck skimming over slick-as-ice playing surface. Break through your opponent's defense and score! Perforated plastic playing surface about 24x11 in.; sturdy metal frame. Two concealed fans assure constant, even air cushion. Two pucks, two goalies, two scoreboards. Order six "C" batteries on page 377. Hong Kong.
48 G 14870—Ship. wt. 5 lbs. 4 oz. **10⁹⁹**

1980 Sears

Action Games for the sports-minded family

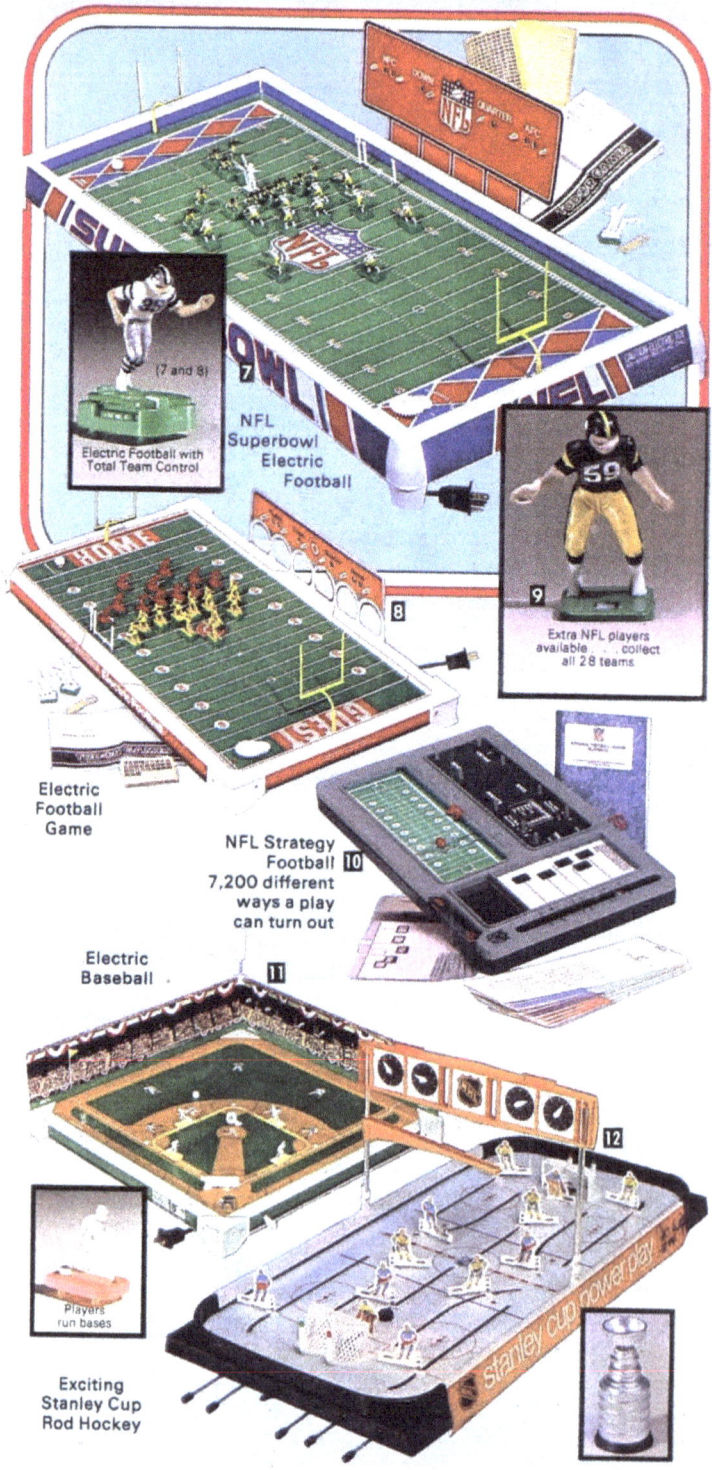

(1) Giant 30-game Cube Table... a whole game room in a box. Sets up into a game table in a few minutes. Made of colorful reinforced fiberboard; supports up to 150 lbs. Doubles as a table, hassock, or seat. Triple varnished to resist stains; wipe clean with damp cloth. Includes parts, illustrated instructions for chess, checkers, backgammon, Michigan Rummy, horse race, 25 others. 86 playing pieces store inside. 15x15x15 in. high.
AGES, ORDER INFO: 8 years and up. Unassembled, instructions.
49 N 61106C—Shipping weight 4 pounds $15.29

(2) Fast Shot Aerial Target Game. Aim the airplane firing control stick. Fast repeater fire action. Shoots pellets. Automatic scoring. Bells ring, target spins, when it is scored.
CONSTR: 10x8¼x7-in. high plastic arcade. Completely enclosed.
AGES, ORDERING INFO: 5 years and up. Imported.
49 N 62785—Shipping weight 1 pound 14 ounces......... $9.69

(3) Space Target Game. Shoot the balls at the 3 hinged colorful, space motif, knock-down targets. Easy-load flip-up targets.
CONSTRUCTION: 12x10½-in. durable plastic flip-up targets. 4 light plastic balls, repeating action easy-load pistol. Imported.
AGES, ORDERING INFO: 3 years and up.
49 N 62787—Shipping weight 15 ounces $6.69

(4) Winnie-the-Pooh Ball Darts. Soft balls stick like magic.
CONSTRUCTION: 17x15-inch high brightly colored nylon cloth target; polyurethane backing. 3 Velcro® covered plastic balls.
AGES, ORDERING INFO: 3 years to adult.
49 N 62722—Shipping weight 6 ounces........... $5.89

(5) Carrom® Set. Shoot the rings... make them bounce into net pockets.
CONSTR: Reversible 26-in. square wood-grained laminated hardboard panel, molded high-impact styrene corners. 4 net pockets.
ACCESSORIES: 2 ring shooters for accuracy, speed, power; carrom rings; numbered discs; dice, spin tops, ten-pins; 100 game rule book. Replacement rings sold separately below.
AGES, ORDERING INFORMATION: 7 years to adult.
49 N 62127C—Shipping weight 7 pounds 11 ounces $12.49

(6) Revolving Stand for (5). Plated steel arms, legs.
ORDER INFO. Unassembled. Instructions included. 24½ in. high.
49 N 62128C—Shipping weight 1 pound 13 ounces $4.29

Carrom® Board and Revolving Stand. Save $2.00. Separate prices total $16.78. Includes (5) and (6) described above.
49 N 62129C2—Shipping weight 9 pounds 8 ounces.... $14.78

Replacement Carrom Rings (not shown). Package of 29.
49 N 65149—Shipping weight 6 ounces ....Package $2.49

(7 and 8) Electric Football Games. Total Team Control dial in base of each player determines movement. Players in 5 poses. Switch on game and field vibrates. Speed control dial. Automatic timer starts and stops with each play.
ELECTRICAL INFO: UL listed; 110-120-v., 60-Hz. AC. 6 watts. 5-foot cord. Not recommended for ages under 8½ years.
AGES, ORDER INFO: 8½ years and up. Partly assembled. Instr.

(7) NFL Superbowl Electric Football... officially licensed product. Metal playing field 31⅝x17⅜x3 inches high. 3½-inch high adjustable scoreboard. 22 plastic figures in official team colors, plus 2 triple-threat quarterbacks, magnetic 10-yard marker with movable chain marker, rubber balls, down marker.
49 N 62034CD—Shipping weight 8 pounds $25.99

(8) Electric Football Game. Metal field 26⁷⁄₁₆x15⅜x1⅞ inches high. Scoreboard with stand, 24 plastic players, 10-yard marker and down indicator.
49 N 65536C—Shipping weight 3 pounds 14 ounces $14.99

(9) Extra NFL Players... officially licensed product. 11 figures per team. 4 or 5 teams in divisions in official team colors. Figures attach to Total Control Base (not included).
49 N 62699D—4 AFC Central Division Teams
49 N 62701D—4 NFC West Division Teams
4-team Set. Shipping weight 5 ounces .... Each $9.99
49 N 62702D—5 AFC East Division Teams
49 N 62703D—5 AFC West Division Teams
49 N 62704D—5 NFC East Division Teams
49 N 62705D—5 NFC Central Division Teams
5-team Set. Shipping weight 6 ounces .... Each $11.99

(10) NFL Strategy Football... officially licensed. 40 offensive and 12 defensive alignments. 7,200 ways a play can turn out. Probability selector gives statistical results. Plastic playing surface. 14½x9 in. Scoreboard, NFL playbook, automatic timer.
AGES, ORDERING INFORMATION: 8½ years to adult.
49 N 6526D—Shipping weight 2 pounds 6 ounces $16.99

(11) Electric Baseball. Pitch, field using 2 spring-action levers; opponent hits with spring-action bat, switch on vibrating field to send players around bases. 19⁵⁄₁₆x19⁵⁄₁₆-in. metal field. 4 base runners. 7⅞-in. high grandstand and scoreboard.
ELECTRICAL INFO: UL listed, 110-120-v., 60-Hz. AC. 6 watts. 5-foot cord. Not recommended for ages under 8½ years.
AGES, ORDER INFO: 8½ years and up. Partly assembled, instr.
49 N 65072C—Shipping weight 3 pounds 10 ounces $14.99

(12) NHL Stanley Cup Hockey. Officially licensed product. Push rods in or out to move players; twist rods to spin players for "slapshots". Playing field 36x18x3½-in. 12-plastic figures, score tower, puck dropper, auto. puck ejector, Stanley Cup Replica.
AGES, ORDER INFO: Partly assembled. Instr. 8 yrs. to adult. If mailed, takes 15-lb. rate ... see page 336.
49 N 62298L—Shipping weight 11 pounds 11 ounces ... $19.99

THERE ARE 23 OTHER PAGES OF GAMES FOR FAMILY FUN IN SEARS FAMILY-GAME CENTER... PAGES 643 THROUGH 667

1980 Montgomery Ward

Push-button basketball

Electronic Battleship

Extra NFL players. Collect all 28 teams!

1981 Montgomery Ward

1981 Sears

Capture the excitement of the sports arena with tabletop Sports Games

(1) **NFL team Figures**... officially licensed product. 11 figures per team. 4 or 5 teams in divisions in official team colors. Figures attach to Total Control Base (not included).
4-team Sets
49 C 62699—AFC Central Div.
49 C 62701—NFC West Div.
Shipping weight 5 oz........ $10.49
5-team Sets
49 C 62702—AFC East Div.
49 C 62703—AFC West Div.
49 C 62704—NFC East Div.
49 C 62705—NFC Central Div.
Shipping weight 6 oz........ $12.49

(2) **NFL Electrical Football Game**. fast, exciting and action-filled
Officially licensed product. Total team Control dial in base of each player determines movement. Switch on game and field vibrates. Speed control dial. Automatic timer starts, stops with each play.
CONSTR. Metal playing field 31⅝x17⅜x3 in. high. 3½-in. high adjustable scoreboard. 22 plastic figures in official team colors in 5 poses, plus 2 triple-threat quarterbacks, magnetic 10-yd. marker with movable chain marker, rubber balls, down marker.
ELEC. INFO: UL listed; 110–120-volt, 60-Hz. AC. 6 watt. 5-foot cord.*
AGES. ORDER INFO 8½ years and up. Partly assembled. Instructions.
49 C 62034C—Shipping weight 7 pounds $24.99

(3) **Electric Baseball**. Pitch, field using 2 spring-action levers; opponent hits with spring-action bat, switch on vibrating field to send players around bases. 19⁴⁄₁₆x19⁵⁄₁₆-in. metal field. 4 base runners. 7⅝-in. high grandstand and scoreboard.
ELECTRICAL INFO: UL listed, 110–120-v., 60-Hz. AC. 6 watts. 5-foot cord*.
AGES. ORDERING INFORMATION: 8½ years and up. Partly assembled, instructions included.
49 C 55072C—Wt. 3 lbs. 8 oz. ... $14.79

(4) **NHL Stanley Cup Hockey**
Officially licensed product. Push rods in and out to move players; twist rods to spin players for "slapshots". Playing field 36x17x3½ inches. 12 plastic figures, score tower, automatic puck ejector. Stanley Cup Replica.
AGES. ORDERING INFORMATION: Partly assembled. Instructions included. 8 years to adult. If mailed, takes 15-lb. rate. See page 360.
49 C 52298L—Wt. 8 lbs. 8 oz. ... $22.99

(5) **Carrom® Game**. Shoot the rings, make them bounce into 4 net pockets. 2 ring shooters for accuracy, speed, power; rings; numbered discs; dice, spin tops, ten-pins, 100 game rule book. Replacement rings sold separately below. Reversible 26¾x26¾x1⅞-in. square wood grained laminated hardboard panel, molded high-density polyethylene corners.
AGES AND ORDERING INFORMATION: 7 years to adult.
49 C 62127C—Wt. 7 lbs. 12 oz. .. $13.99

(6) **Revolving Stand for (5)**. Plated steel arms, legs. 24½ inches high.
ORDERING INFORMATION: Unassembled. Instructions included.
49 C 62128C—Wt. 1 lb. 14 oz. $4.49

Carrom® Board and Revolving Stand. Save $2.60. *Separate prices total $18.48.* Incl. (5), (6) above.
   Shipping weight 9 lbs. 10 oz.
49 C 62129C $15.88

Replacement Rings for Carrom® game (not shown). Package of 29.
   Shipping weight 6 ounces.
49 C 65149 .... Package $2.99

*Not recommended for ages under 8½ years.

1982 Sears

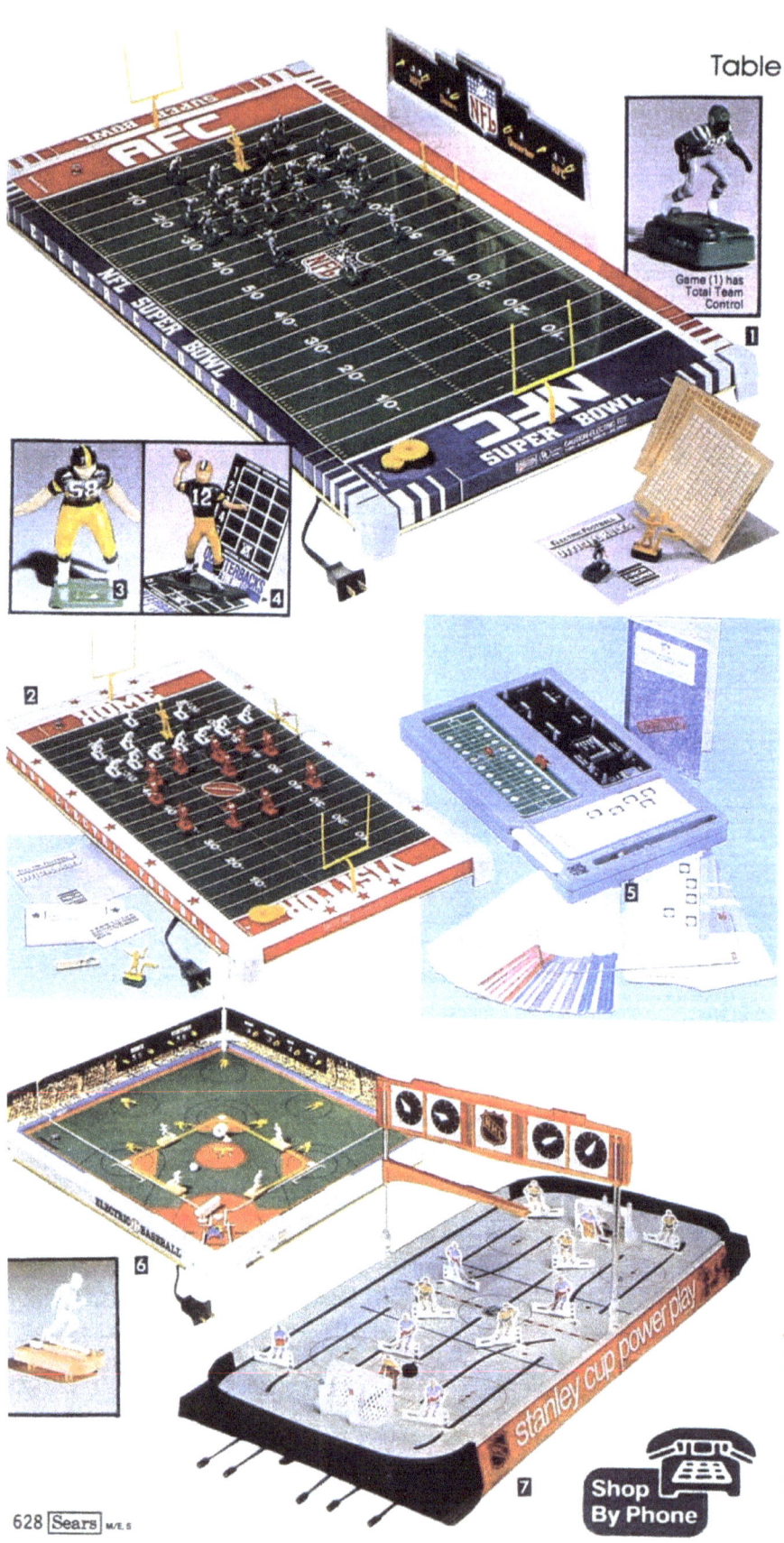

1982 J.C. Penney

Action Games for Good Sports

NFL Electronic Football with Total Team Control

A NFL Super Bowl

B NFL Football

NFL Teams come with players molded in 5 different positions

A & B Total Team Control Football. Just set the wheel in the base of each player for direction, adjust speed control on the field, switch on the game, and watch the vibrating metal field start the action. Automatic timer starts and stops with each play. Includes 22 plastic players (enough for 2 full teams) molded in 5 different 3-D poses in NFL team colors. Triple-threat quarterback can kick, pass, and run. Magnetic down marker with movable 10-yard marker, magnetic ball, plastic goal posts, 4 plastic goal-line flags. Scoreboard on grandstand in paperboard. Easy-to-apply numbers, 2 through 89. Ages 8½ and up.
[A] NFL Super Bowl. 16¼x32½ in.-wide playing field 36x19⅛x2¹⁄₁₆ in. high.
XU 923-0004 A—Delivery weight 5 lbs . . . . Set **24.49**
[B] NFL Football. 13x24 in.-wide playing field 27x16½x4x2 in. high
XU 923-0012 A—Delivery weight 4 lbs . . . . Set **17.99**
Additional NFL Teams. All 28 teams in official team colors with decals. Each 11-player team included with sets [A] and [B] has both black and white players molded in 5 different 3-D poses. Order teams by conference and Division. Del. wt. 0.80 lb. each.
National Conference Teams:
XU 924-9855 A—Eastern (Cardinals, Cowboys, Eagles, Giants, Redskins)............ **13.99**
XU 925-9045 A—Central (Bears, Buccaneers, Lions, Packers, Vikings)............ **13.99**
XU 925-9052 A—Western (Falcons, 49'ers, Rams, Saints)............ **10.99**
American Conference Teams:
XU 924-9889 A—Eastern (Bills, Colts, Dolphins, Jets, Patriots)............ **13.99**
XU 924-9897 A—Central (Bengals, Browns, Oilers, Steelers)............ **10.99**
XU 925-9060 A—Western (Broncos, Chargers, Chiefs, Raiders, Seahawks)............ **13.99**

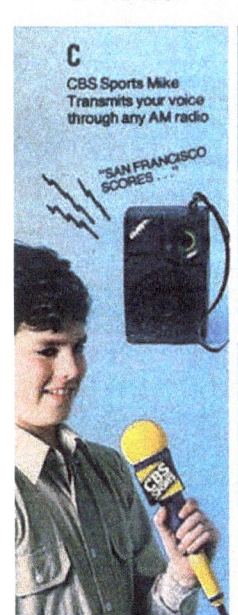

C CBS Sports Mike Transmits your voice through any AM radio

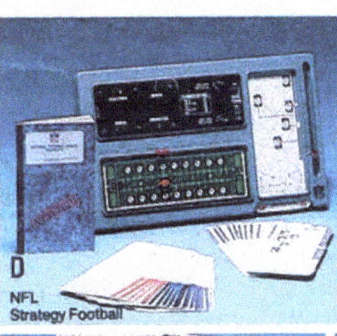

D NFL Strategy Football

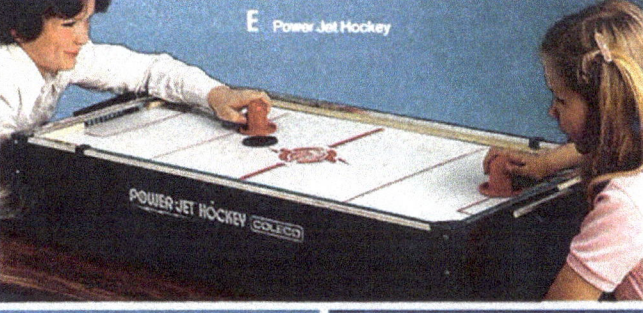

E Power-Jet Hockey

F Pivot Pool

G Super Soccer

H NHL Stanley Cup® Hockey

C Feel Like A Real Sportscaster with CBS Wireless Microphone. Transmit your voice through any AM radio. Includes flexible antenna. Uses one 9-volt battery—not included, sold on page 523. FCC approved. Plastic. Imported from Hong Kong.
XU 652-0076 A—Delivery weight 0.80 lbs **8.99**

D NFL Strategy Football. The Probability Selector determines statistically correct results for the plays you mastermind. Set includes plastic game case with adjustable scoreboard, play selector, and 14¼x9-in. playing field with football marker. In addition, there's an NFL playbook, and 40 offensive and 12 defensive play diagrams. For 2 or more players, ages 8½ years and up.
XU 924-9848 A—Delivery weight 2.40 lbs . . Set **19.49**
See special NFL index on page 439

E The Action's Fast and Furious with Power-Jet Hockey.* Air is forced through tiny holes on playing field, forming a cushion of air that makes the puck really fly! Lively bumpers for fast rebounds. There's a realistic playing surface of white Masonite® fiberboard with red lines. 2 red plastic controllers, 2 plastic pucks. Built-in scoreboard. Laminated wood cabinet is 44x20 in. wide overall. Brown plastic corner braces, chrome-plated metal top rail. Not fully assembled—assembly requires a screwdriver and pliers. For 2 players, ages 8 and up. Warranted by manufacturer, see page 427.
XU 925-5878 A—Delivery weight 30 lbs **38.49**

F Pivot® Pool. Pivoting shooter swivels. Adjust for hard or soft shot, and fire the cue ball from the pivot. Automatic ball return. Table 19x32½ in. long. Pressed-paper top, plastic frame. Full set of balls and a rack. Ages 8 to adult.
XU 923-7843 A—Delivery weight 11.25 lbs **27.49**

G Super Soccer. Exciting, fast-moving fun for the whole family. Each team controls 5 ready-for-action players, including a goalie. Steel soccer ball can be passed forward to score. Made of heavy-gauge plastic. Playing field measures 25x19 in. wide, 4¹⁄₁₆ in. high. For 2 teams of 1 or 2 players, ages 8½ to adult.
XU 652-0332 A—Delivery weight 6 lbs **21.99**

H NHL Stanley Cup® Tabletop Hockey. Ten rods control player action—two levers control goalies. Styrene-coated playing surface. Pro-style goals with automatic puck ejectors. Working 2-sided score tower with puck drop, penalty box. Miniature Stanley Cup is metallicized plastic. Stick-on uniform decals of 18 NHL teams. 36x18x18 in. high overall. Wood composition, steel, plastic. Easy to assemble. 2 players, ages 8 years and up.
XU 924-4153 A—Delivery weight 9 lbs **26.49**

* UL listed for 110-120 volts, AC.
Caution: electric toy—see note on page 534.

1983 Sears

Table top Sports Games

(1 and 2) Electric Football Games. the biggest game of the year in your "stadium". Players in 5 poses. Switch game and field vibrates. Speed control Automatic timer starts and stops with play.
ELEC. INFO: UL listed. 110–120-v. 60 AC. 6 watts. 5-foot cord. Not recommen for ages under 8½ years.
FOR AGES: 8½ years and up.
ORDER INFO: Partly assembled. Inst tions included. Warranted by Tudor, for free copy, see page 376.

(1) NFL Super Bowl Electric Footbal ficially licensed product. Large metal p ing field measures 35 1/16 x 18 3/4 x 1 1/8 in high. 3½ inch high adjustable scorebo 22 plastic figures in official team co plus 2 triple-threat quarterbacks. T Team Control dial in base of each player termines movement. Magnetic 10-y marker with movable chain marker, felt and down indicator.
49 N 62708C—Wt. 5 lbs. 4 oz. ...$26

(2) Electric Football Game. Metal f measures 26 7/16 x 15 3/8 x 1 1/8 inches high. plastic players with bases that determ player movement. Scoreboard pads, yard marker and down indicator.
49 N 62709C—Wt. 3 lbs. 12 oz. ..$15

(3) NFL Team Figures. Collect all 28 teams. Officially licensed product. 11 ures per team in official team colors. 4 teams in divisions. Figures attach to all t bases (not included).
ORDER INFO:
4-team Sets
49 N 62699—AFC Central Division
49 N 62701—NFC West Division
Shipping weight 5 ounces..........$12
5-team Sets
49 N 62702—AFC East Division
49 N 62703—AFC West Division
49 N 62704—NFC East Division
49 N 62705—NFC Central Division
Shipping weight 6 ounces..........$14

(4) Quarterbacks of the NFL. Officia censed product. Incl. all 28 NFL quar backs with team standings boards ... can be used with games (1 and 2) abov
ORDER INFO:
49 N 62706—Wt. 5 oz. $9

(5) NFL Strategy. Outwit your oppon as you call the plays in a classic gam strategy. Officially licensed product. 40 fensive and 12 defensive alignments p duce 7,200 ways a play can turn out. Pr bility selector gives statistical results. Pla playing surface 14½x9 in. Scoreboard. playbook, automatic timer.
FOR AGES: 8½ years to adult.
ORDER INFO:
Shipping weight 2 pounds 6 ounces.
49 N 62711 ....$19

(6) Electric Baseball. Enjoy America's vorite pastime. Pitch and field with 2 spr action levers. Opponent hits with spring tion bat. Switch-on vibrating field se players around bases. 19 5/16 x 19 5/16-in. al playing field. 4 base runners. 7 7/8-in. h grandstand.
ELEC. INFO: UL listed. 110–120-v. 60 AC. 6 watts. 5-foot cord. Not recommen for ages under 8½ years.
FOR AGES: 8½ years and up.
ORDER INFO: Partly assembled. Instr tions included. Warranted by Tudor, write for free copy, see page 376.
Shipping weight 3 pounds 8 ounces.
49 N 65C72C $15

(7) NHL Power Play Hockey. "Skat your team to victory and win the Stan Cup. Officially licensed product. Push r in and out to move players; twist rods spin players to score. Playing field meas 36x17x3½ in. high. 12 plastic figur score tower, puck dropper and automa puck ejector included.
FOR AGES: 8 years and up.
ORDER INFO: Partly assembled. Instr tions included. If mailed, takes 15-lb r ... see page 376.
Shipping weight 8 pounds 12 ounces.
49 N 62298L ....$26.

1984 Montgomery Ward

I Rocky Rock 'em Sock 'em™ action playset provides hours of fun helping Rocky and Mr. "T" duke it out. Be the first player to knock your opponent's block off and win!
48 G 51151—Ages: 7 and up. Ship. wt. 5 lbs. 8 oz. 18.88

J Pac Man™ Magnetic Maze™ from Tomy. Pac Man tries to gobble up the magnetic pieces without getting trapped by the monsters in the maze. You control Pac Man by using the joystick provided with the game. Ages: 5 and up.
48 G 51122—Ship. wt. 1 lb. 12 oz. 9.77

K Deluxe Scrabble Crossword Game. Now, the perennial favorite comes in a deluxe edition! This elegant version is the perfect step-up for devoted Scrabble players. The playing surface spins smoothly on a built-in turntable base, and the squares are recessed so tiles won't slide out of place. Comes complete with playing board with revolving base, 100 hardwood tiles, 4 tile racks, scorepad and a drawstring bag to hold tiles; rule booklet. For 2, 3 or 4 players, ages 8 to adult.
48 G 14420—Ship. wt. 4 lbs. 10 oz. 19.97

L Super Bowl Electric Football Game. Realistic looking NFL® game brings the Super Bowl right into your own home! Each player has his own I.D. number and can be posed 5 different ways. Sturdy steel game board is 16x32 in. Adjustable scoreboard with automatic timer. UL listed. Comes with safety plug and a 5-foot cord. Ages: 8 and up.
48 G 14552—Ship. wt. 5 lbs. 14 oz. 27.88

M Quiz Wiz™ question and answer computer for kids. With cartridge/Quiz Book No. 1; 1001 Questions and Answers. Machine tells you if you're right or wrong. No. 28 Quiz Wiz cartridge sold separately below. Uses one 9-volt battery (not included, order page 490). 6 and up Ship. wt. 8 oz. *Order after Oct. 1, 1984.*
48 G 14408—Ages: 6 and up. Ship. wt. 8 oz. 19.99

Quiz Books for (M) above. *State item no.:* 03–Movies & TV, 05–Trivia, 23–Words, 26–The Bible, 28–Ripley's, 30–Funny Animals.
L 48 G 51601—Ship. wt. 8 oz. .... any 2 for 11.88

N Set of 2 games teach patriotic trivia. "See the U.S.A." is a fast-paced game that has the players peg in cities and points of interest on the map by their starting letter. Speed is important—sand timer controls turns. "Know Your America:" 7 categories of trivia test your knowledge of the U.S. Over 300 questions and answers. For 4 players.
48 G 14792—Ages: 10 through teens. Ship. wt. 3 lbs. 13 oz. .... set 9.99

1985 Sears

A winning game plan...

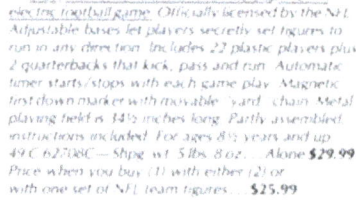

Save $4 on game (1) when you also buy item (2) or a set of NFL team figures

When you can't get home for Christmas, send Christmas home with Ship-a-Gift. See page 538.

1. Enjoy half-time fun with the NFL Super Bowl electric football game. Officially licensed by the NFL. Adjustable bases let players secretly set figures to run in any direction. Includes 22 plastic players plus 2 quarterbacks that kick, pass and run. Automatic timer starts/stops with each game play. Magnetic first down marker with movable yard chain. Metal playing field is 14½ inches long. Partly assembled, instructions included. For ages 8½ years and up.
49 C 62708C — Shpg. wt. 5 lbs. 8 oz. .. Alone **$29.99**
Price when you buy (1) with either (2) or with one set of NFL team figures ... **$25.99**

2. Get your favorite Quarterbacks of the NFL. Collect these figures alone or for use with NFL Game (1) above. Officially licensed by the NFL, set includes all 28 NFL quarterbacks in team colors, plus a team standings board.
49 C 62706 — Shpg. wt. 5 oz. ... **$9.99**

NFL team figures (not shown) are officially licensed by the NFL. Sets include 11 figures per team, all in official colors. Figures attach to all team bases of NFL Game (1) sold above.

Division	Catalog Number	Shpg. wt.	Price
4 TEAM SETS			
AFC Central	49 C 62699	5 oz.	$12.99
NFC West	49 C 62701	5 oz.	12.99
5 TEAM SETS			
AFC East	49 C 62702	6 oz.	$14.99
AFC West	49 C 62703	6 oz.	14.99
NFC East	49 C 62704	6 oz.	14.99
NFC Central	49 C 62705	6 oz.	14.99

3. Take "time out" for the NBA BAS-KET game. There's no penalty for playing overtime with this official NBA version of the fast moving game. Featuring all the popular NBA teams, the game lets players control the shots with mechanical levers. Comes complete with court, scoreboard, game ball, free team decals. For 2 to 6 players or teams. For ages 5 years to adult.
49 C 62516. Wt. 2 lbs. 4 oz. .. **$7.99**

4. You'll get a kick out of Subbuteo™ table soccer. Now you can have all the action and excitement of the world's most popular soccer game in your own home. Includes table size cloth playing surface, two 11-man teams and accessories for play. Also includes a 1986 World Cup color poster. For 2 to 4 players. For ages 7 to 17 years.
49 C 62825. Wt. 1 lb. 4 oz. ... **$19.99**

5. Face-off for fun with NFL Stanley Cup Play-off Hockey. Realistic features include overhead scoreboard, automatic puck dropper, plastic netted goals with goal "light" indicators, and remote action puck ejector. Includes two teams in official NFL uniforms, powered by smooth gliding control rods for easy maneuvering. Also includes a Stanley Cup replica. Authentic hockey graphics add to fun. 16x21½x4 inches tall. For ages 8 years to adult.
49 C 62295L — Shipping weight 11 pounds... **$37.99**

1986 Sears

Score one for fun

Quarterbacks of the NFL (2)
Cut 50%

Save $4 on game (1) when you also buy item (2) or a set of NFL team figures

1 Enjoy half-time fun with this officially licensed NFL Super Bowl electric football game. Adjustable bases let players secretly set figures to run in any direction. Includes 22 plastic players plus 2 quarterbacks that kick, pass and run. Automatic timer starts/stops with each game play. Magnetic first down marker with movable 'yard' chain. Metal playing field is 34½ inches long. Partly assembled.
For ages 8½ years and up.
49 N 62708C—Shpg. wt. 5 lbs. 8 oz. Alone $29.99
Price when you buy (1) with either (2) or with one set of NFL team figures $25.99

2 Get your favorite quarterbacks of the NFL! Collect these figures alone or for use with NFL Game (1) above. Officially licensed by the NFL, set includes all 28 NFL quarterbacks in team colors, plus a team standings board. Was $9.99 in 1985 Christmas Catalog, page 585.
49 N 62706—Shpg. wt. 5 oz. $4.99

NFL team figures (not shown) are officially licensed by the NFL. Sets include 11 figures per team, all in official colors. Figures attach to all team bases of NFL game (1) sold above.

Division	Catalog Number	Shpg. wt.	Price
4-team sets			
AFC Central	49 N 62699	5 oz	$12.99
NFC West	49 N 62701	5 oz	12.99
5-team sets			
AFC East	49 N 62702	6 oz	$14.99
AFC West	49 N 62703	6 oz	14.99
NFC East	49 N 62704	6 oz	14.99
NFC Central	49 N 62705	6 oz	14.99

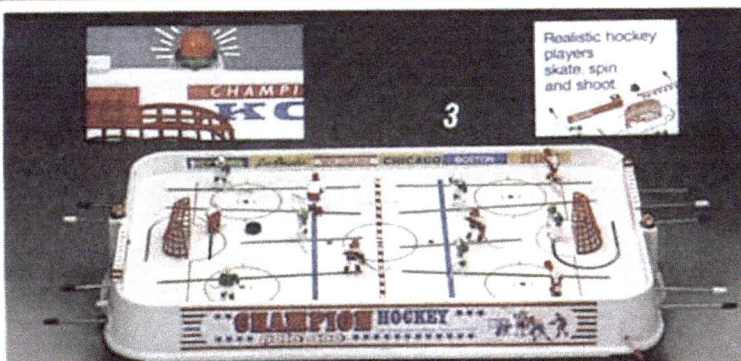

Realistic hockey players skate, spin and shoot.

3 Talk about realism! This Champion table-top ice hockey game has 3-dimensional hockey players. Red lamp lights up when scoring. Conewheel system assures fast movement, accurate passes and hard shots. Includes 12 molded plastic players powered by smooth gliding control rods for easy maneuvering. 33½x20¼x3¾ in.
For ages 5 years to adult.
49 N 62717C—Shpg. wt. 9 lbs. $59.99

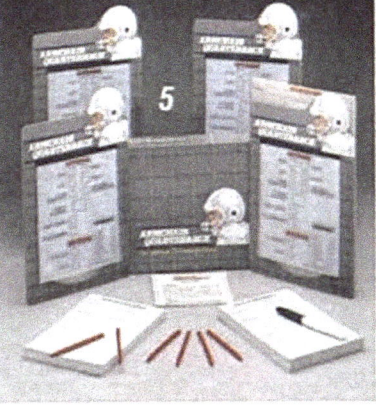

4 Take 'time out' for the NBA BAS-KET game. There's no penalty for playing overtime with this official NBA version of the fast moving game. Featuring all the popular league teams, the game lets players control the shots with mechanical levers. Comes complete with court, scoreboard, game ball. Team decals included. For 2 to 6 players or teams.
For ages 5 years and up.
49 N 62516—Shpg. wt. 2 lbs. 4 oz. $8.99

5 Play football with the pros. Imagine sitting in front of your television and calling the plays. Match your strategy against the players, coaches and your friends. Score by guessing the plays before they happen. Includes 4 playing boards, double roster pad, scoreboard, 6 styluses, felt scoring pen and rules.
For ages 8 years and up.
49 N 62718—Shpg. wt. 2 lbs. 5 oz. $12.99

1987 J.C. Penney

B & C Total Team Control Football. Set player's direction and speed, then vibrating metal field starts the action. Automatic timer. Includes 22 plastic players (enough for two full teams). Triple-threat quarterback can kick, pass, and run. Paperboard scoreboard. Easy-to-apply numbers. UL listed for 110-120 volts AC. For ages 8 years and up.

B. NFL Super Bowl. 16¼x32½ in. wide playing field. 35x18¾x1¾ in. high overall.
XU 923-0004 A—Del. wt. 4.90 lbs. 32.99

C. Additional NFL Teams. All 28 teams in official team colors with decals. Each division has four or five complete 11-player teams. Each team has both black and white players molded in five different 3-D poses.

4-Team Sets. Del. wt. each 0.80 lb.
AFC Central—XU 924-9897 A 12.99
NFC West—XU 925-9052 A 12.99

5-Team Sets. Del. wt. each 0.80 lb.
NFC East—XU 924-9855 A 14.99
NFC Central—XU 925-9045 A 14.99
AFC East—XU 924-9889 A 14.99
AFC West—XU 925-9060 A 14.99

D. Football Card Collection Kit. Double D-ring vinyl album with 6 plastic topload card collector pages, 50 individual card sleeves, 50 hard to find out-of-print Topps® collector cards. 50 Years of NFL Excitement book. Football Superstars book, poster, price guide and storage box. For ages 6 years to adult.
XU 672-2839 A—Del. wt. 3.75 lbs. 15.99

E. NFL VCR Quarterback Game. Playing board interacts with tape of actual NFL play footage. 2-hour VHS tape, playing board, markers, playing pieces dice, and play cards. For ages 8 years and up.
XU 672-2565 A—Del. wt. 3 lbs. 39.99

A. NFL Huddles Team Mascots. Acrylic plush. Vinyl football and helmet, plastic accessories. 7 in. high. Teams: 10 Bears; 04 Cowboys; 07 Redskins; 25 (S.F.) 49'ers; 06 Rams; 03 Dolphins; 11 Raiders; 27 Giants; 28 Patriots; 39 Broncos. State team number and name. Imported from Korea. Ages 5 years and up.
XU 672-1732 B—Del. wt. 0.75 lb. .... Ea. 13.99

F. Topps® 1987 Football Card Set. Complete collection of 396 cards. For ages 6 years to adult.
XU 672-2821 A—Del. wt. 1.75 lbs. .... Set 12.99

G. NFL Hall of Fame Cards. Set of each player elected to NFL Hall of Fame through 1986. 135 cards in all. For ages 6 years to adult.
XU 672-2847 A—Del. wt. 0.50 lb. .... Set 8.99

H. Football Card Value Pack. 225 mint-condition football cards including limited editions. "Fifty Years of NFL Excitement" book. For ages 6 years to adult.
XU 672-2854 A—Del. wt. 1.50 lbs. 9.99

I. NFL Strategy Game. Features 48 offensive and 15 defensive football plays giving over 10,000 different results. Includes NFL playbook, dice, and strategy cards. Comes in easy-to-carry vinyl-covered wooden case. 17¾x9½x2⅛ in. Imported from Taiwan. For ages 8 to adult.
XU 672-2862 A—Del. wt. 4 lbs. 35.99

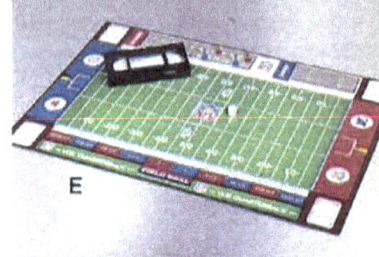

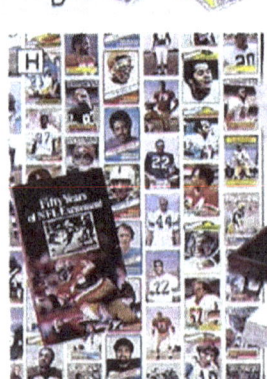
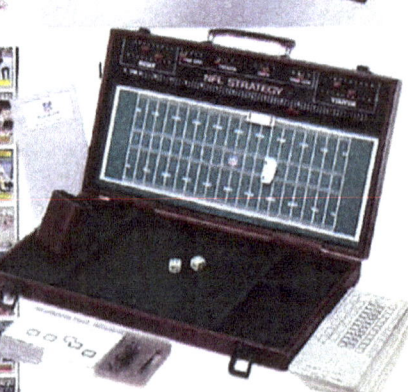

1988 Sears

Can't make it to the game? Get your

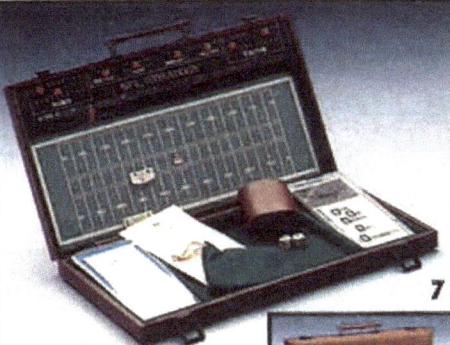

Football strategy game will test you over and over with more than 10,000 outcomes

Save $15 $34.99

Save $2 on Bear Huddle-ette (6)
$7.99 when you also buy (5)

1 thru 5 Cuddly Huddles for play or display. Team mascots have soft plush bodies, nylon tricot football, vinyl helmets. 7 in. high. Ages 3 years and up.

Huddles shown at left
- (1) 49 N 62762—Broncos
- (2) 49 N 62769—Vikings
- (3) 49 N 62766—Seahawks
- (4) 49 N 62764—Redskins
- (5) 49 N 62753—Bears

Huddles not shown
- 49 N 62763—Cowboys
- 49 N 62765—49ers
- 49 N 62767—Dolphins
- 49 N 62768—Bengals
- 49 N 62770—Browns

Wt. 2 lbs. 12 oz. . . Each $12.99

6 Bear Huddle-ette adds real spirit! 8 in. high.
49 N 62761—Wt. 12 oz. . . Alone $9.99
When you also buy (5). . . $7.99

7 Are your strategies as good as the pros? The ultimate football strategy game has 48 offensive and 15 defensive plays for over 10,000 different results. Includes 48-page playbook. Vinyl-covered carrying case. 2 players, ages 8 and up.
49 N 62784—Wt. 4 lbs. . . $39.99

8 No pain, but you still gain! VCR Quarterback has all the excitement without the bruises. Over 400 great NFL plays on one 2-hour VHS tape. All NFL teams are represented. For 2 players, ages 8 and up. Was $49.99 in our 1987 Wish Book For Kids.
49 N 62697—Wt. 3 lbs. . . $34.99

9 The next Super Bowl will be held in your home! Electric Super Bowl game is 34½ inches long. Includes scorecards. Not recommended for ages under 8.
49 N 62708—Wt. 5 lbs. 8 oz. . . $39.99

NFL team figure sets (not shown) include 11 figures per team. Can be used with Super Bowl game (9) above.

Division	Teams	Catalog No.	Wt.	Set
AFC Central	4	49 N 62699	5 oz.	$12.99
NFC West	4	49 N 62701	5 oz.	12.99
AFC East	5	49 N 62702	6 oz.	14.99
AFC West	5	49 N 62703	6 oz.	14.99
NFC East	5	49 N 62704	6 oz.	14.99
NFC Central	5	49 N 62705	6 oz.	14.99

The perfect game companion, Huddles will never miss a game... or win a bet!

Punt, pass and kick with pro strategies
$39.99

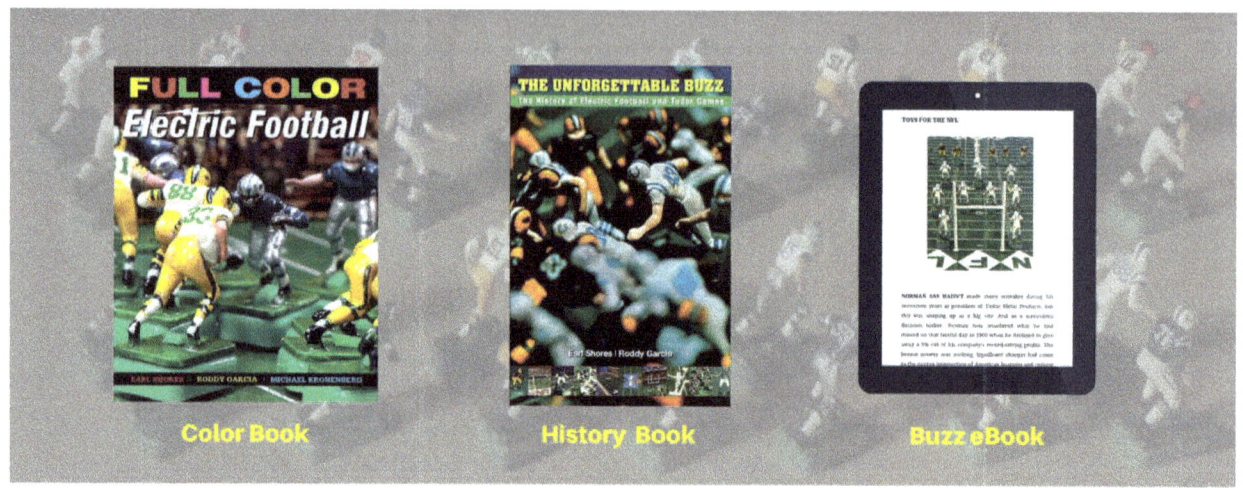

More About Electric Football

To learn more about Electric Football and its history be sure to check out our books *The Unforgettable Buzz: The History Of Electric Football and Tudor Games* (2013) and *Full Color Electric Football* (2015). *The Unforgettable Buzz* is an unparalleled 652-page compendium of the Electric Football story. The book has garnered great praise, earning a 4.8 star (out of 5) Amazon rating.

Full Color Electric Football is an epic oversized 8" x 10" all-photo journey through Electric Football's colorful past. Over 250 beautiful images bring childhood memories to life – the book earned the No. 3 spot on the 2015 UniWatch/ESPN Holiday Gift Guide List. And please visit our media sites:

theunforgettablebuzz.com
www.facebook.com/theunforgettablebuzz
fullcolorelectricfootball.com
twitter.com/TheUBuzz

Between these sites you'll find over five years' worth of Electric Football posts and stories, including rare images and thoughtful insights into the most iconic sports toy ever created. Our Top 20 All-Time Electric Football Games is a great place to get acquainted with *The Unforgettable Buzz*. We guarantee that there is nowhere else like our site on the entire web -- or in the entire universe! And Electric Football is still alive and well. You can pick up brand new NFL games, teams, and accessories – as well as our books – from the **Tudor Games** website:

tudorgames.com

About The Authors

Earl Shores, Roddy Garcia, and Michael Kronenberg have spent the last five years documenting the story of Electric Football. The *Electric Football Wishbook* is their third book, finishing off an Electric Football trilogy that includes the critically acclaimed *The Unforgettable Buzz* and *Full Color Electric Football*.

Nearly two decades worth of research went into these books, including rare conversations and materials from Electric Football inventor and former Tudor Games President Norman Sas, and former Tudor designer and Director of Product Development Lee Payne. The meticulous work of Shores, Garcia, and Kronenberg has produced a "toy story" whose thoroughness is unrivaled.

Game Index

1969 Alden: Tudor NFL No. 620; Tudor No. 501-2; Gotham NFLPA G-895

1955 Ward: Gotham All-Star G-880

1955 Spiegel: Tudor Tru-Action No. 500

1956 Sears: Gotham Electro-Magnetic G-940

1958 Ward: Gotham G-880

1962 GMC: Tudor Sports Classic No. 600; Gotham G-880

1962 Spiegel: Retailer specific Tudor No. 500 w/grandstand

1962 Sears: Gotham NFL G-1500; Gotham G-940

1962 Ward: Tudor Sports Classic No. 600; Ward specific No. 500 w/grandstand (possibly a No. 501)

1963 Sears: Gotham NFL G-1500; Gotham NFL G-1400; Gotham NFL G-890S; Pressman Vibro-Power Football

1963 Ward: Tudor SC No. 600; Ward specific No. 500 w/grandstand

1964 Sears: Gotham NFL G-1500; G-1400; G-890S

1964 Ward: Tudor SC No. 600; Tudor No. 500

1964 Aldens: Gotham NFL G-890; G-1500

1965 First: Tudor No. 500; Tudor SC No. 600

1965 Sears: Gotham NFL G-1500; NFL Big Bowl G-1503-S; G-890S

1965 Ward: Tudor No. 500; Tudor SC No. 600

1966 Sears: Gotham NFL Big Bowl G-1503-S; NFL G-1500; G-890S

1966 Ward: Tudor "Accordion" No. 600; Bayshore Stop-Action Football; Tudor No. 500

1967 Sears: Gotham Big Bowl G-1504-S; Tudor NFL No. 613; Gotham G-883

1967 Ward: Tudor Ward-specific NFL No. 620; Tudor No. 500

1968 Sears: Gotham Big Bowl G-1504-S; Gotham G-883; Tudor NFL No. 613

1968 Ward: Tudor Ward-specific NFL No. 620; Tudor No. 501-2; Tudor NFL No. 619

1968 Otasco: Tudor Generic No. 500 Super Bowl

1969 Penney: Gotham NFLPA Super Dome G-1512; Tudor No. 501-2

1969 Sears: Sears Tudor NFL No. 630-633 Super Bowl; Gotham NFLPA Super Dome G-1512; Tudor NFL No. 618

1969 Ward: Tudor Ward-specific NFL No. 620; Tudor No. 501-2; Tudor NFL No. 619

1970 Sears: Sears Tudor NFL No. 630-633 Super Bowl; Tudor NFL No. 618; Tudor NFL No. 510

1970 Ward: Tudor Ward NFL No. 627; Coleco Pro Stars 5765-66; Tudor NFL No. 619

1970 Penney: Gotham NFLPA Super Dome G-1512; Tudor No. 501-2

1970 Aldens: Tudor NFL AFC No. 610; Gotham Joe Namath G-812

1971 Sears: Sears Tudor NFL Super Bowl No. 630-633; Tudor NFL No. 618; Tudor NFL No. 510

1971 Ward: Tudor Ward NFL No. 627; Tudor NFC No. 520; Tudor NFL No. 615.

1971 Sears (Coleco): Sears Exclusive Coleco Executive Command Control Electric Football (model # unknown)

1972 Spiegel: Coleco Command Control 5795; Coleco Pro Stars 5765; Tudor No. 501-2

1972 Sears (Coleco): Sears Exclusive Coleco Executive Command Control Electric Football (model # unknown)

1972 Sears (Munro): Day-Nite Electric Football 4202

1972 Sears: Sears Tudor NFL Super Bowl No. 633; Tudor NFL No. 618; Tudor NFL No. 510

1972 Ward: Tudor Ward NFL No. 627; Tudor Ward NFL No. 627L

1972 Penney: Coleco Command Control 5795; Tudor NFL No. 635; Coleco Pro Stars 5755

1972 Penney: Gotham Floor Model Electric Football G-883L

1973 Aldens: Coleco Command Control Touchdown Football 5775

1973 Sears (Munro): Day-Nite Electric Football 4201 (Special Sears Floor Model)

1973 Sears: Sears Tudor NFL Super Bowl No. 633; Tudor NFL No. 618; Tudor NFL No. 515

1973 Ward: Tudor Ward NFL No. 627L; Tudor Ward NFL No. 627; Tudor NFL No. 515

1973 Penney: Coleco Super Action Command Control Football 5780; 5779

1973 Penney: Tudor NFL No. 635; Gotham G-883L

1974 Sears: Sears Tudor NFL Super Bowl No. 633-635; Tudor NFL No. 635; Tudor NFL No. 515

1974 Ward: Tudor Ward NFL No. 627; Tudor NFL No. 635; Tudor NFL No. 515

1974 Penney: Tudor NFL Championship No. 655; Tudor NFL No. 635; Tudor NFL No. 515

1975 Penney: Tudor NFL Championship No. 655; Tudor NFL No. 635; Tudor NFL No. 515

1975 Sears: Sears Tudor NFL Super Bowl No. 633-635; Tudor No. 500

1975 Ward: Coleco Command Control 5795

1976 Sears: Sears Tudor NFL Super Bowl No. 633-635; Tudor No. 500

1976 Ward: Coleco Command Control 5795

1976 Penney: Tudor NFL Championship No. 655 (two teams); Tudor NFL No. 635; Tudor NFL No. 515

1977 Penney: Tudor Super Bowl No. 660; Tudor NFL No. 515

1977 Sears: Sears Tudor NFL Super Bowl No. 635; Tudor No. 500

1977 Ward: Coleco Command Control 5795

1978 Sears: Sears Tudor NFL Super Bowl No. 635; Tudor No. 500

1978 Ward: Tudor Super Bowl No. 660

1980 Sears: Sears Tudor NFL Super Bowl No. 635; Tudor No. 500

1980 Ward: Tudor Super Bowl No. 660

1981 Ward: Tudor Super Bowl No.660

1981 Sears: Sears Tudor NFL Super Bowl No. 635

1982 Sears: Tudor NFL Super Bowl No. 600; Tudor No. 500

1982 Penney: Tudor Super Bowl No. 660; Tudor NFL No. 520

1983 Sears: Tudor NFL Super Bowl No. 600

1984 Ward: Tudor NFL Super Bowl No. 600

1985 Sears: Tudor NFL Super Bowl No. 600

1986 Sears: Tudor NFL Super Bowl No. 600

1987 Penney: Tudor NFL Super Bowl No. 600

1988 Sears: Tudor NFL Super Bowl No. 600

www.ingramcontent.com/pod-product-compliance
Lightning Source LLC
Chambersburg PA
CBHW061119010526
44112CB00024B/2921